Canva

FOR BEGINNERS

A Step-by-Step Guide to Master Canva's Tools and Graphic Design With Confidence, Even If You're Just Getting Started

Jules Harper

Contents

Introduction

In August 2013, Canva launched with a bold mission to make graphic design accessible to everyone. Within the first year, over 750,000 users signed up, drawn in by its simple, drag-and-drop interface and beautiful templates. What once required professional software and years of training could now be done in minutes by anyone – no design experience needed!

But was the path to success really this easy?

Not even close!

Before Canva became a household name, its founder, Melanie Perkins, faced over 100 rejections. The idea for Canva had been in the making since 2007, when Perkins, then a university student in Australia, struggled with complex design software. She saw her peers at university struggle to learn professional design programs, which were often expensive and difficult to use.

Driven to make their vision a reality, Perkins and her co-founder, Cliff Obrecht, launched a small project called *Fusion Books* – an online platform that allowed students to create their own yearbooks. It was a success, but Perkins knew the potential was much bigger.

> "Our goal was to take the entire design ecosystem, integrate it into one page, and then make it accessible to the whole world," she said.

So, she began pitching Canva to investors. But time and time again, she was turned down. Investors didn't believe a small startup from Australia could disrupt the world of design. Others doubted that graphic design could ever be truly simplified.

But she refused to give up.

After refining her pitch and improving the platform, Perkins finally caught the attention of Bill Tai, a venture capitalist who saw Canva's potential. With the right backing, Canva officially launched in 2013 – and changed the design world forever – and for the better.

Today, Canva is well on its way to fulfilling its mission of making design accessible to everyone. From individuals creating social media posts to businesses designing presentations and marketing materials, Canva has empowered millions with an easy, intuitive platform that removes the barriers of traditional graphic design.

While Canva has undoubtedly simplified the design process, many users still only scratch the surface of what the platform has to offer.

It is more than a tool to access quick templates. In fact, its features range from animated graphics and video editing to brand kits and collaboration tools. The platform has the potential to transform how businesses, educators, marketers, and students approach design on a professional level.

This book will guide you through these untapped possibilities and help you unlock the true power of Canva. Get ready to turn your ideas into beautifully executed designs!

What Is in This Book for You?

Canva for Beginners is your step-by-step guide to mastering the art of graphic design, even if you've never picked up a design tool. If you are looking to create stunning visuals without the steep learning curve of traditional design software, you are in the right place.

In this book, you can expect to

- learn the basics of using Canva's user-friendly interface, understand the key tools and features, and start creating your first designs in minutes.
- explore ways to create social media posts, animations, videos, presentations, flyers, and much more with Canva's wide range of templates and design elements.
- discover essential design principles such as color theory, typography, and layout.

- understand how to use Canva for branding and marketing through logos, business cards, and marketing material.

By the end of this book, you'll be not only proficient in Canva's tools but also confident in your ability to create designs that communicate your message effectively, stand out in a crowded digital landscape, and look professional, all while having fun with the process. Whether you're designing for personal projects or building a brand, Canva has the tools to bring your ideas to life, and this book will show you how to make the most of them.

With 93% of communication happening through visuals, are you ready to enhance your impact using Canva?

Understanding the World of Canva

For years, graphic design felt exclusive. It was locked behind expensive software, technical skills, and the belief that only professionals could create something truly impressive. What about the rest of us? We hesitated. We second-guessed. We stuck to the plain and uninspired visuals because we were unsure if we had the *eye* or the *talent* to design anything worthwhile.

However, this quote from Joseph Chilton Pearce changed how I looked at design, and it might help you, too:

> "To live a creative life, we must lose our fear of being wrong".

Canva helps us do exactly that.

It removes the barriers, the hesitation, and the fear of making mistakes. With its intuitive drag-and-drop interface, professionally designed templates, and beginner-friendly tools, Canva makes creativity accessible to everyone. You don't need a degree in design. You don't need years of experience. You simply need an idea and the willingness to explore. The potential is limitless!

In this chapter, we'll dive into what makes Canva so powerful, how it transforms the design process, and why it has become an essential tool for millions worldwide. By the end, you won't just understand Canva – you'll be ready to create without any constraints.

What Is Canva and How Does It Redefine Design Accessibility?

Canva is a versatile web-based graphic design platform that opens doors to a vast collection of professionally designed templates, an extensive library of fonts, images, and icons, and powerful editing tools that effortlessly bring ideas to life.

I like to refer to Canva as a *creative playground*. It is a space where imagination meets simplicity and anyone can design confidently without spending months mastering traditional design software.

Most people on their way to learning Canva have one question on their minds: *Is it worth spending time learning Canva when I could invest that same time in learning a professional design tool?* It's a valid question, especially with so many advanced design tools available. However, the answer lies in understanding the differences in both usability and purpose. Let's address this before we move forward.

Comparing Canva to Professional Design Tools

Feature	Canva	Adobe Photoshop	Adobe Illustrator	Adobe InDesign
Learning curve	easy, intuitive drag-and-drop interface	steep learning curve, requires extensive training	steep learning curve, requires advanced skills	steep learning curve, requires extensive training
Best for	quick designs, social media graphics, presentations, marketing materials	high-end photo editing, complex image manipulation	logo design, vector art, illustrations	layout-heavy projects, brochures, magazines
Flexibility and customization	limited customization for pre-designed templates	high flexibility, complete creative control	highly flexible for vector-based designs	detailed control over text and layout
Collaboration	easy collaboration in real-time	limited collaboration features	limited collaboration features	limited collaboration features
Tools and features	templates, icons, fonts, stock photos, simple editing tools	complex tools for photo manipulation, filters, and effects	advanced tools for vector drawing and precision	advanced tools for vector drawing and precision
Cost	free, with a Pro version available at a low cost	high subscription cost	high subscription cost	high subscription cost

Canva may not replace professional software for highly specialized tasks, but it is more than sufficient for a vast majority of everyday design needs, which makes it a go-to solution for accessible and creative expression.

So, to answer the question above, I would say that if your goal is to create effective, polished designs quickly without the need for extensive technical skills, Canva is an excellent choice. Professional tools may be necessary for more intricate design needs, but for 90% of everyday projects, Canva provides everything you need to succeed in the world of design.

What Makes Canva So Special?

Canva's success is primarily due to its diverse range of intuitive features that meet the needs of a wide variety of design projects. Let's take a look at the unique features of Canva:

Customizable Templates

At the heart of Canva's appeal is its library of customizable templates. These templates are a springboard for creativity and provide a solid foundation to enhance your confidence in design. This feature proves invaluable for those who may be intimidated by a blank Canva page and unsure where to start.

A variety of design layouts can help you understand how visual elements can be effectively arranged. This knowledge then inspires new ideas and encourages you to try different features.

Powerful Collaboration Features

Canva's real-time collaborative features are another standout element. Unlike traditional design software that requires multiple file versions and long email threads, Canva allows real-time collaboration and streamlines the entire design process.

With Canva, you can invite team members to view, edit, or comment on a design instantly. Whether it's a classroom setting where students contribute to a group presentation or a business team developing marketing materials, collaboration can take place smoothly.

Drag-And-Drop Interface

Canva's intuitive drag-and-drop interface is one of the reasons why it has become a go-to platform for so many people. All you have to do is drag elements like text, images, or icons from the sidebar and drop them onto your page. It's as simple as that!

Here is how it works:

- Need to add a new element to your design? Just drag it over from the sidebar and place it anywhere on your page.
- Once you have placed an element, you can easily adjust it by resizing, rotating, or changing the color—all with only a few clicks.
- Canva helps you keep your designs clean and neat. As you move elements, smart guides appear to help you align everything perfectly without extra effort.

Access to Stock Photos, Icons, and Illustrations

As a user, you have access to millions of free and premium stock photos, illustrations, icons, and design elements, all available directly within the platform. This means you don't have to spend hours searching through various stock photo websites or purchasing expensive images from third-party providers.

You can easily search for the perfect image you are looking for and drag it directly into your design, which saves you hours of searching and organizing. All images, icons, and elements are high in quality. After you have chosen the perfect elements for your design, you can even resize, crop, adjust the colors, or layer them with other elements to create something unique to your vision.

Design Animation and Video Editing Capabilities

Contrary to what most people believe, Canva offers more than static graphics. You can create animated designs and engaging video content effortlessly. Find all the essential tools to add movement and personality to your designs without needing advanced video editing skills.

Easy-To-Use Animation Tools

With just a click, you can animate text, images, graphics, and even entire pages. Canva provides a range of animation styles, such as:

- fade-in and fade-out
- slide and bounce
- zoom and pop
- typewriter effect

User-Friendly Video Editing Features

Canva takes video creation to the next level with its built-in video editor that allows you to produce professional-looking videos without the complexity of traditional editing software. Here's what you can do:

- **Cut and trim videos:** Easily remove unwanted parts of your footage to keep your content concise and engaging.
- **Add transitions:** Smoothly move between clips with stylish transitions for a polished look.
- **Choose background music and sound effects:** Pick from Canva's collection of royalty-free music or upload your own to set the perfect mood for your content.
- **Include text and motion graphics:** Overlay text, animated graphics, and stickers to create compelling storytelling elements.
- **Resize for different platforms:** Effortlessly adjust your video's dimensions to fit TikTok, Instagram Reels, YouTube, or any other platform.

Flexible Export Options

Canva also allows you to export designs in various formats to meet different needs. You can download your creations as PNG, JPEG, PDF, or even GIF files, depending on what you're using the design for. For presentations or social media posts, Canva makes it simple to adjust your design for various platforms, such as Instagram, Facebook, or Twitter.

Canva's high-quality export options ensure that your designs look crisp and clear no matter where you share them.

The Benefits of Using Canva for Content Creation

Besides having access to the powerful features mentioned above, Canva offers several benefits that make content creation easier, faster, and more efficient. Let's take a look at each:

Ease of Use

Canva's ease of use stands out as a primary benefit. Its intuitive design allows users without any design background to navigate effortlessly. Unlike traditional design software with a steep learning curve, Canva's drag-and-drop feature simplifies the process. This ease is particularly beneficial for novices who want to create content without spending weeks learning new skills.

Suppose you are a student tasked with creating a big presentation. Instead of struggling with complicated design software, you open Canva and instantly access an array of professionally designed templates, adjust them with a few clicks, and produce a polished presentation in no time. Just like that, you have a sleek presentation that looks like it was made by a pro. This simplicity allows you to focus on delivering your message rather than getting lost in design complexities.

Creative Freedom

For beginners, the creative freedom Canva provides is liberating. In the past, creating eye-catching designs required understanding complex software. Now, with Canva, you can access thousands of templates and elements. You can experiment with fonts, colors, images, and layouts without concern for making irreversible mistakes.

Canva encourages exploration and trial, making design a creative playfield rather than a daunting task. If you need to design a social media post for your small business, you'd need advanced knowledge of layers, masks, and blending modes to create engaging visuals with traditional tools. In Canva, you can simply select a template, adjust the colors to match your branding, swap out elements, and add animations—all in minutes. You have complete creative control without the technical hassle.

Time-Saving

Rather than starting from scratch, you can select from thousands of ready-made templates to save time. These templates

- provide a strong starting point for your designs.
- help you maintain a professional aesthetic.
- ensure consistency in branding and marketing materials.
- allow you to create high-quality content in minutes.

Cost-Effective Alternative to Expensive Software

Cost-effectiveness also plays a pivotal role in Canva's appeal. Traditional graphic design software often requires costly licenses and periodic updates. In contrast, Canva offers a free tier with ample features to create impressive designs.

For small businesses and freelancers maintaining tight budgets, Canva's affordable premium options unlock even more advanced tools. Think about a nonprofit organization aiming to create promotional materials. With Canva, they save on hiring external designers and direct funds toward their mission instead. The Pro version of Canva allows users to scale their needs without financial strain.

Automatic Resizing for Different Platforms

Canva's Magic Resize feature lets you automatically adjust your designs for different platforms. With one click, you can convert a Facebook post into an Instagram story, a

YouTube thumbnail, or a LinkedIn banner to make sure your visuals are optimized for every platform without extra effort.

Constantly Grow and Learn

Canva offers tutorials and blogs that support users at every stage. These resources provide insights and spark creativity. As a new user, you will be welcomed into a community focused on shared learning.

What starts as simple template customization soon evolves into creating unique designs from scratch. As you build confidence, you naturally move beyond templates and develop your own creative style.

Accessibility Across Multiple Devices

Canva is a cloud-based platform, which means you can access it anytime, anywhere, or on any device. This is beneficial for those who need flexibility in where and when they design. Whether on a desktop, tablet, or phone, Canva's platform provides consistent functionality.

Canva's approach to design has effectively lowered the barriers and democratized the design field. It has empowered users to not only consume content but create, share, and make their voices heard visually. The wave of user-generated content from diverse socio-economic backgrounds testifies to these advantages!

Back to You

Now that you understand what makes Canva different from other design platforms, it is time to think about how you can put it to work for yourself. Start by asking yourself these questions:

- ***Which of Canva's benefits stands out to me the most?*** Is it the ease of use, the vast template library, the collaboration features, or something else? Identifying what excites you will help you make the most of the platform.
- ***How can I incorporate Canva into my workflow?*** Whether you're a

student, entrepreneur, content creator, or someone who simply loves designing, think about where Canva can help streamline your projects.

- ***What's my first step in using Canva effectively?*** Do you need to create an account, explore templates, or set up brand colors and fonts?

Taking the first step makes the learning process smoother. In the next chapter, I'll walk you through the process of creating and setting up your Canva account for success!

Getting Started With Canva

Say goodbye to complicated software downloads and endless updates to access the latest features of a design tool. Canva changes the game by offering an entirely web-based platform that lets you design from anywhere, at any time. To use it on a desktop, tablet, or even smartphone, all you need is an active internet connection, and you're ready to create!

This chapter is your guide to taking your very first steps on Canva. From setting up your account and understanding the differences between the free and Pro plans to customizing account settings and selecting the correct dimensions for your projects, you'll gain the essential knowledge to start designing. Let's get you set up!

How to Create an Account on Canva

Creating a free Canva account is your first step to unlocking a world of possibilities in graphic design without professional experience. It's simple and begins right on Canva's homepage. Follow these steps to create an account:

Step 1: Visit the Canva Website or Download the Application

- Open your preferred web browser and go to www.canva.com.
- If you're using a mobile device, download the Canva app from the Apple App Store (iOS), Google Play Store (Android), or AppGallery (Huawei). The app provides the same functionality as the web version, with the added convenience

of designing on the go.

Step 2: Click on "Sign Up"

- On the Canva homepage, locate the "Sign up" button in the top right corner.
- Click it to begin the registration process.

Step 3: Choose a Sign Up Method

Canva offers multiple ways to sign up:

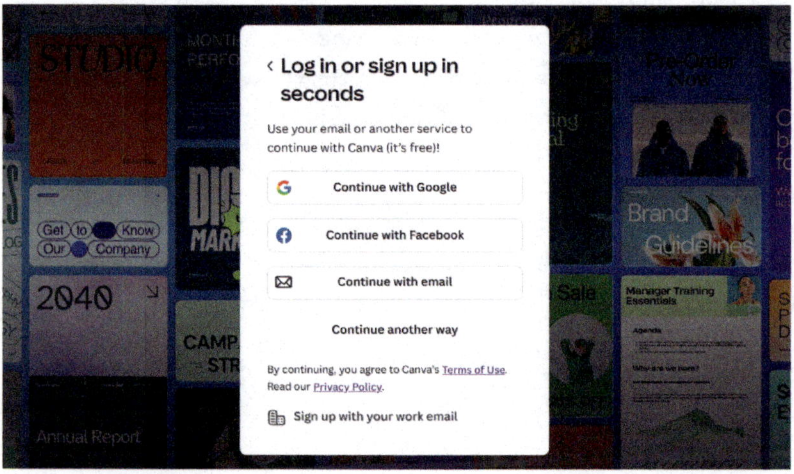

- **Email address:** Enter your email, create a password, and click "Sign up."
- **Google account:** Click "Continue with Google" and select your Google account.
- **Facebook account:** Click "Continue with Facebook" and log in to your Facebook profile.
- **Continue with other options:** Click on "Continue with other options" to view more login choices, including continue with Apple, Google, Microsoft, or Clever. You can even log in through your mobile phone using the web version.

- **Work email:** Click on "Sign up with your work email" for a professional Canva experience.

Step 4: Confirm Your Email (If Signing Up With Email)

- Canva will send a verification email to the address you provided.
- Open the email and click the confirmation link to activate your account.
- Check your spam or junk folder if you don't see the email.

Step 5: Select Your Account Type

After verification, Canva will ask about your intended use. You can choose from a few different options:

- personal (for individuals and hobbyists)
- small business (for entrepreneurs and startups)
- large business (for corporate branding and marketing)
- nonprofit or charity (for organizations looking for design support)
- education (for teachers, students, and schools)

Selecting the correct category helps Canva suggest relevant templates and tools suited to your needs.

Step 6: Set Up Your Profile (Optional but Recommended)

- Add a profile picture (especially useful for team collaborations).
- If using Canva for work, customize your brand settings by uploading your logo and setting brand colors.
- Explore the dashboard to familiarize yourself with available tools and features.

And just like that, you've successfully created your Canva account!

Canva Free vs. Canva Pro: Which Version Suits Your Needs Best?

Canva offers two main account options: Canva Free and Canva Pro. While both versions provide access to Canva's user-friendly design tools, the Pro plan unlocks advanced features that enhance efficiency, branding, and customization. Understanding the differences will help you decide which plan best suits your needs.

Canva Free: A Solid Start for Beginners

The free account is good enough to let you explore a multitude of templates, ranging from social media graphics to presentations and posters. It offers access to a vast library of photos, icons, and fonts, giving you the tools needed to start designing right away.

The free version of Canva is perfect for individuals who want to create professional-looking designs without spending a dime. It provides

- access to thousands of templates.
- basic design tools for adding text, images, and graphic elements.
- limited access to stock photos and elements.
- an ability to collaborate with others on projects; however, advanced collaboration tools are not available.
- options to download files in PNG, JPG, and PDF formats.
- 5GB of cloud storage space.

Canva Pro: Unlocking Advanced Features

For those wanting to expand their design options without limitations, investing in a Canva Pro account could be a game-changing deal. One of the biggest perks is access to unlimited premium templates, which can significantly enhance your designs' visual appeal. The Pro account is more than just aesthetics; it provides a range of exclusive benefits, including the following:

- extensive stock library with 100+ million high-quality photos, videos, audio tracks, and graphics
- brand kit for consistency that allows you to save your brand's fonts, colors, and logos in one place
- magic resize to instantly resize a design for different platforms without having to adjust the dimensions manually
- background remover that removes the background from images in just one click to create cleaner, more professional designs
- premium fonts and effects
- collaborative tools to create folders and share templates within a team
- 1 TB of cloud storage
- more download options to export designs with transparent backgrounds, high-resolution files, and additional formats

Let's take a look at the side-by-side comparison of Canva Free versus Canva Pro:

Feature	Canva Free	Canva Pro
Templates	basic selection	unlimited access to 610,000+ premium templates
Stock photos and elements	limited	100+ million premium assets
Magic resize	not available	available
Background remover	not available	available
Brand kit	not available	available
Cloud storage	5 GB	1 TB
Download formats	PNG, JPG, PDF	transparent PNG, GIF, MP4, SVG
Collaboration tools	basic sharing	advanced workflow and approval tools
Cost	free	$15 per month or $120 per year

If you ask me, Canva Free is ideal for individuals, students, and occasional designers who need a simple and effective way to create visual content. Canva Pro is best for businesses, marketers, influencers, and teams that require premium assets, branding tools, and time-saving features.

If you're unsure, Canva offers a 30-day free trial of Pro. It will allow you to explore the premium features before committing.

Fool-Proof Account Customization Settings

Once your account is set up and you have chosen between the free and Pro version, the next step is to master the customization options within account settings. Adjusting these settings will empower you to meet your personal or business needs.

Personalizing Your Account Settings

Canva offers several customization options to enhance user experience. You can

- adjust the language or choose a preferred language for your interface.
- set up your Canva theme, including contrasts and color schemes, to match your style.

- enable two-factor authentication for added security.

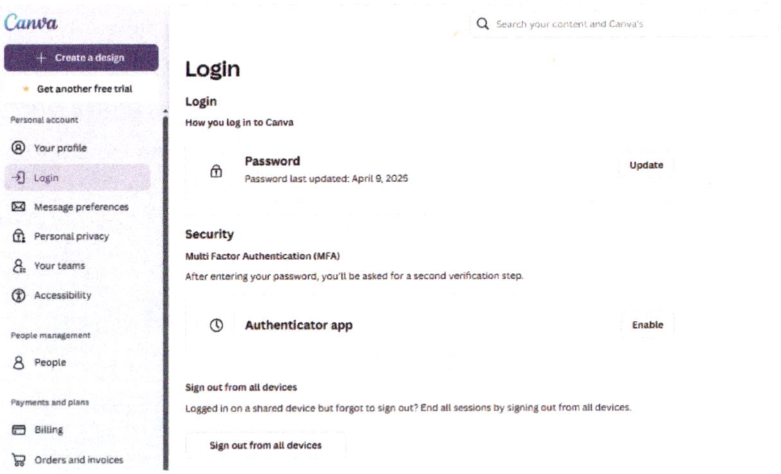

Taking a few minutes to set up these preferences will make your design experience more efficient and secure.

Managing Privacy and Collaboration Settings

Privacy and collaboration settings are crucial, especially if you're part of a team, so make sure they are adjusted. They allow you to

- control access to your designs and dictate who can view or edit your designs.
- add or remove members from your team as needed.
- limit actions such as editing, commenting, or downloading your files.

Navigating Canva's Support Options

Canva simplifies troubleshooting with built-in support options. In the settings panel, you can

- find tutorials and step-by-step guides to solve common issues.
- reach Canva's customer service for technical help.

- get answers to frequently asked questions.

Keeping Your Workspace Organized

Effective account management can dramatically increase your design efficiency. Keeping your workspace organized helps maintain focus and productivity. You should

- develop a habit of archiving projects you no longer work on. It reduces clutter and helps you zero in on active designs.
- create folders for better organization, and group projects by type or client, if applicable.

Regular review of account benefits is essential to maximize your usage. As Canva rolls out new features or updates, be proactive in exploring and incorporating them into your workflow. Staying resourceful in this way ensures you're always getting the most out of what you've paid for—especially if you're on a Pro account.

With the basics of account setup and management covered, it's time to look forward to mastering the Canva dashboard and exploring file types.

Navigating Canva's Dashboard and Understanding Custom Sizing

Right after you log into your Canva account, you will be directed to the Canva home, also known as the dashboard. This is your creative command center, where you can start new projects, access past designs, explore templates, and manage your brand assets.

Understanding how to navigate the dashboard efficiently will help you streamline your workflow and maximize your design potential. Let's break it down for you:

The Main Navigation Panel

Located on your absolute left-hand side, you have the main navigation panel. This panel, which also allows you to open or close the menu, will act as your map and help you access your saved designs, templates, brand kits, and more.

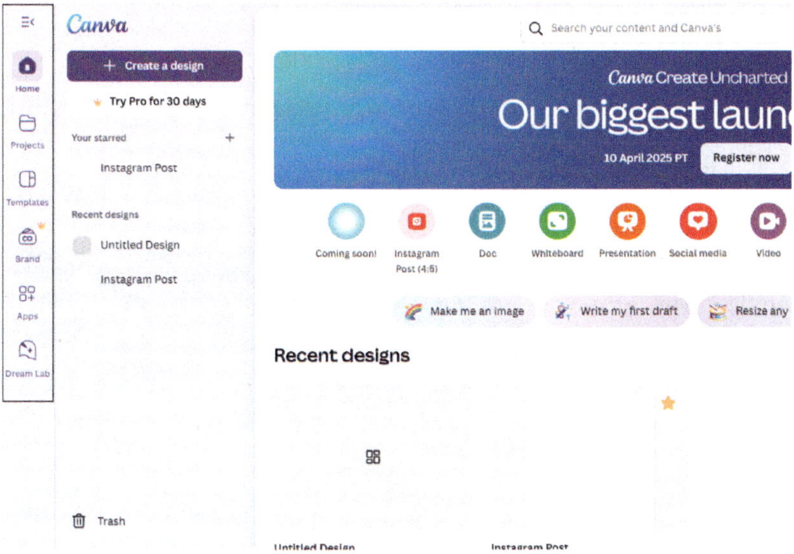

Here are the essential features that deserve your attention:

- **Home:** Clicking on this will return you to the main home page.
- **Projects:** You can view your saved designs, folders, and brand assets here.
- **Templates:** This will allow you to browse from thousands of pre-designed templates. The main niches include business, social media, education, video, marketing, print products, cards, and invitations.
- **Brand (Pro):** This Pro feature easily lets you store logos, fonts, and colors for consistent branding.
- **Apps:** Access third-party integrations like stock photos, AI tools, and social media schedulers here.
- **Dream lab:** An AI-driven image creation tool that enables you to easily transform your ideas into stunning visuals.

The Menu

On the main navigation bar, you'll see a hamburger menu (three lines). Click on that, and you will be able to access:

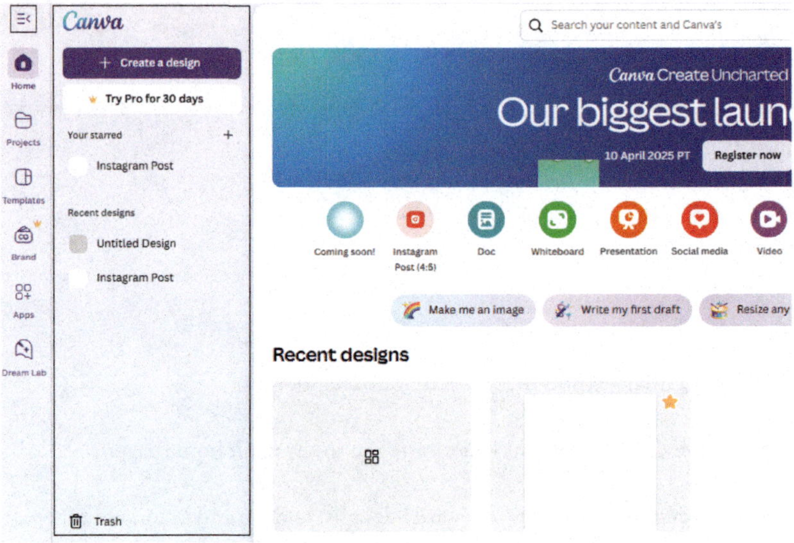

- **Create a design:** Clicking on this will result in a pop-up to choose and get started on your design right away.
- **Get a free trial:** If you are using a free plan, you can sign up for a free Pro trial using this.
- **Your starred and recent projects:** This gives you easy and quick access to any of your starred or recent projects.
- **Trash:** This works just like "Recently Deleted." You can restore them (if it was there for less than 30 days) or delete them permanently from here.

The Search Bar

At the top of the dashboard, you'll see a search bar. This tool allows you to

- search for templates.

- locate your previous projects.
- discover graphics, icons, and images to use in your creations.

To the right of the search bar are settings and notifications. You can use them as you need.

Design Options and Custom Sizes

On the main home screen, there are a number of design options laid in front of you. Simply click on the available categories such as "Doc," "Whiteboard," "Presentation," "Social media, "Video," or "Website." Each option presents you with a set of templates tailored to specific needs to help you create content quickly and efficiently.

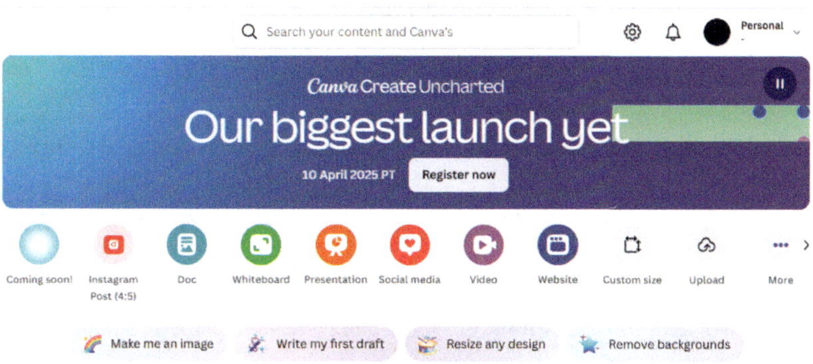

However, if you want to start from scratch, it is a good idea to opt for "Custom size." This feature allows you to manually enter the exact width and height of your design in pixels, inches, millimeters, or centimeters. Choosing the correct dimensions is the first step to creating a fantastic design.

How to Choose the Right Dimensions

Each platform has specific size recommendations to ensure your design displays correctly without being cropped or distorted. Here are some common sizes used across various platforms:

Design type	Recommended sizes
Social media	• Instagram post: 1080 × 1080 px (square) • Instagram story/reel: 1080 × 1920 px (vertical) • Facebook cover photo: 820 × 312 px • Facebook post: 1200 × 630 px
Marketing and print materials	• Poster (Small): 11 × 17 inches • Poster (Large): 24 × 36 inches • Business Card: 3.5 × 2 inches • Flyer: 8.5 × 11 inches
Presentations and website design	• PowerPoint slide (16:9): 1920 × 1080 px • YouTube thumbnail: 1280 × 720 px • Website banner: 2500 × 800 px

There are quite a few benefits of choosing a custom size:

- ensures your design fits perfectly without unwanted cropping
- maintains high resolution, avoiding pixelation in print or digital formats
- adapts to specific project needs, whether for social media, marketing, or personal use

If you are unsure about dimensions, Canva also provides size presets to make the process easier.

Back to You

Now that you know how to set up your Canva account and how to choose the right design size, it is time to put that knowledge into action! Canva's flexibility allows you to create anything from social media posts to full-scale marketing materials, and the best way to learn is by doing.

Here are three action steps to get started right now:

1. If you haven't already, sign in and explore the dashboard to get familiar with the available options.
2. Decide what you want to create – a social media post, a flyer, or a business card.

3. Click on "Create a design" and then "Custom size." Here, you can enter your preferred dimensions for your project. Once done, click on "Create new design" to launch your project editor.

These small but meaningful steps will prepare you for what's coming in the next chapter, where we will further discuss Canva's tools and features that help you bring your creative ideas to life!

Mastering Canva's Interface and Tools

Now that you know how to, let's suppose you have chosen a custom size of 1080 × 1080 pixels to design a social media post for a skincare brand showcasing their new product launch on Instagram. What's the next step? Will you start searching aimlessly through Canva's features? How will you know what to do first?

This is where understanding the interface and tools in detail comes in. Instead of feeling lost or overwhelmed, you'll learn how to find a perfect template, choose complementary colors, or add your logos and product images. By the end of this chapter, you will be able to bring any idea in your mind to life through design!

Exploring Canva's Interface After Starting a Design

Once you have started a design in Canva, you'll see a variety of tools, panels, and options designed to help you bring your ideas to life. Let's break down everything you see on your screen so you can navigate it with ease:

The Top Toolbar

The top section of the editor contains essential tools and controls for managing your design. Here's what you'll find:

- **Hamburger menu:** Clicking on "Open menu" lets you access the home icon, Projects, Templates, Brand, Apps, and Dream Lab.

- **File menu:** You can rename your design, upload files, adjust settings, access version history, make a copy, create a new design, or find and replace text.
- **Resize (Pro feature):** This Pro tool lets you change the dimensions of your design if needed.
- **Edit, comment, or view:** Here, you choose the mode of working, that is, editing, commenting, or viewing, based on your needs. By default, you will be able to see an editing button with a pen icon next to it.
- **Undo/redo:** This allows you to revert or reapply changes.
- **Save status:** Canva automatically saves your work, but this indicator lets you know if your progress is up to date.
- **Title your project:** Clicking on the default title at the top allows you to rename your project. It is usually named as "Untitled design." Giving your project a clear, specific name makes it easier to organize and locate later, especially if you're working on multiple designs.
- **Get a free trial (if you are on the free version):** If you want to explore Canva Pro features like Background Remover, Magic Resize, or Brand Kit customization, click the "Get a free trial" button in the top bar to start a free trial. This gives you access to premium templates, tools, and features.
- **Edit access:** You'll also see your profile icon with a plus sign (+) next to it. This feature lets you invite people to join your team via their email addresses.
- **Analytics (Pro feature):** This provides valuable insights into your content's performance. You can view metrics such as views, clicks, or engagement rates.
- **Comment button:** Here, you can get real-time feedback and collaborate. Use this to leave notes for yourself or your team, reply to feedback directly on the design, or tag team members to assign tasks or ask questions.
- **Share button:** This enables collaboration by letting you invite team members, generate a shareable link, or download your design.

Action Steps

1. Start it off by naming your design for easy access. Click on the default tile (usually named "Untitled design") at the top left of the screen and type in something relevant, like "Skincare Product Launch Instagram Post."

2. Before we explore the left sidebar, from the top toolbar, check that your file is in editing mode. If it is in viewing mode or commenting mode, you won't be able to make any changes.

3. Double-check your design settings under the File menu. This is where you can make sure your design is the correct size and that auto-save is on so you don't lose progress.

The Left Sidebar

This is where you'll find all the elements needed to build your design:

- **Design:** Browse pre-designed templates and styles tailored to your chosen format from Design. This is great for inspiration or a quick start. You can even choose your preferred language for the templates.

- **Elements:** Access graphics, icons, shapes, frames, and stickers to enhance your design.

- **Text:** Add and customize headings, subheadings, and body text. You can also explore pre-styled text combinations for a professional, coordinated look.

- **Brand:** If you have a brand kit, you can apply your brand colors, fonts, and logos for a consistent look across all your designs.

- **Uploads:** Upload your own images, logos, or brand assets to personalize your design.

- **Tools:** Add text, insert sticky notes, include tables, and draw lines on your design from here.

- **Projects:** Canva keeps your work organized in Projects, which includes all your past designs, folders, and uploads.
- **Apps:** Explore third-party integrations and extra features like QR codes, mockups, or AI-powered tools.

Action Steps

If you're starting from scratch, follow these steps to build your design:

1. **Choose a background color:** Click on "Background" or select an empty space on your page. Pick a solid color or explore patterns and textures. If you're designing for a brand, use brand colors to maintain consistency.
2. **Find relevant graphics and elements:** Click on "Elements" and search for icons, shapes, or stickers that match your design theme. Drag and drop them onto your page, then resize and position them as needed.
3. **Add and customize text:** Click on "Text" and choose from Headings, Subheadings, or Body Text. Experiment with different fonts, sizes, and effects to match the aesthetic. Adjust the text color to contrast well with the background and other elements.
4. **Move and arrange elements for visual balance:** Drag elements around to create a balanced composition. Use Canva's alignment guides to ensure everything is positioned properly. Layer elements by sending them forward or backward as needed.

If you're working with pre-designed templates, here's what you need to do:

1. **Pick a template that matches your vision:** Click on "Templates" and browse the available designs. Choose one that fits your project's purpose, whether it's an Instagram post, flyer, or presentation.
2. **Customize the existing design:** Swap out placeholder text with your own content. Change colors to match your brand or theme. Replace template images with your own uploads or Canva's stock photos.

3. **Refine and finalize your design:** Adjust fonts and element placements to make it unique. Ensure that all text is readable and well-spaced. Preview your design to check for any last-minute tweaks before saving or sharing.

Main Page

The large, blank area in the center of the screen is where you'll build your design. Here, you can

- drag and drop elements from the left panel onto your design.
- move, resize, and rotate objects freely.
- use layers to arrange elements in front of or behind others.
- apply filters, adjust transparency, or use effects to enhance visuals.

Action Steps

1. After you have added elements from the left sidebar, click on any element to drag it into place. Use the corner handles to resize images or text. Hover near the rotation icon to tilt objects for a dynamic look.
2. Right-click an element and select "Send to back" or "Bring to front" to layer objects properly. You can also use the Position tool (found in the top toolbar after clicking the element) for precise alignment.
3. Click on an image or element to access filters, transparency, and adjustments. Add text effects like shadows, neon, or glitch for extra flair.

The Bottom Toolbar

- **Notes:** Add annotations or reminders for yourself or collaborators, which are ideal for presentations and team projects.
- **Zoom in or zoom out:** Adjust the view to work on finer details or get an overview of your design.

- **Thumbnail view:** See all your pages at a glance.
- **Grid view:** Displays all pages in a structured layout, which is useful for organizing multi-page designs.
- **Present full-screen:** Present your project in full-screen mode.
- **Ask Canva:** Find answers to your questions or get help with anything.

Action Steps

1. Use the Zoom tool to zoom in when working on small details like icons or text. Zoom out to see how your design looks as a whole before finalizing it.
2. Switch to "Thumbnail view" or "Grid view" to manage multiple pages easily.
3. Click the Notes section below your page to add comments or reminders for yourself.

Sharing and Downloading Your Design

Once your design is complete, you'll want to share it with others or download it for use. Canva makes this easy with various options tailored to different needs, whether you're collaborating with a team, posting on social media, or printing a high-quality version.

The Share Button: Collaborate and Get Feedback

The Share button at the top right of the screen allows you to copy the link of your project and invite team members, clients, or collaborators to view or edit your design. You have the following sharing options:

- **Edit access:** Invite team members to edit the design in real time.
- **Commenting access:** Allow others to leave feedback without making direct changes.
- **Viewing access:** Share a read-only version.

Here are some steps to share your design:

1. Click the "Share" button.
2. Enter an email address or copy the generated link.
3. Choose the permission level: "Can edit," "Can comment," or "Can view."
4. Click "Send" or "Copy link" to share.

Tip: If working with a team, use Canva's built-in comments to discuss edits without leaving the platform.

Downloading Your Design

Before downloading, consider the purpose of your design in order to select the correct file type and quality. Here is how you can download your design:

1. Click the "Share" button.
2. Select "Download" from the dropdown menu.
3. Choose a file format.
4. Adjust settings if needed (such as a transparent background for PNG).
5. Click "Download" and save the file to your device.

Choosing the Right File Format

Feature	Best for	Key features
PNG	high-quality images, logos, transparency	lossless quality, supports transparent backgrounds
JPG	website images, social media, email attachments	small file size, no transparency, good for photos with many colors
PDF standard	digital documents (e-books, resumes, reports)	optimized for on-screen viewing, retains clickable links
PDF print	professional printing (flyers, posters, business cards)	high resolution (300 DPI), supports CMYK color, includes bleed/crop marks
MP4 video	animated designs, social media videos	smooth motion, high quality, does not support transparency
GIF	short animations, stickers, website graphics	small file size, looping, limited to 256 colors
PPTX	presentations	editable slides, retains layout and animations for PowerPoint users
SVG	scalable vector graphics (icons, logos, illustrations)	infinite scaling without loss of quality, editable in vector software

Tip: For social media posts, Canva provides optimized sizes for platforms like Instagram, Facebook, and LinkedIn. Simply choose the correct preset or resize your design (Pro feature) before downloading.

Publishing Directly From Canva

Canva allows you to post directly to various platforms. You can generate a template link, copy the project link to the clipboard, or even create a public link. There are options to send your design to your phone or move the project to another folder. But it doesn't end there!

Platforms where you can publish directly through Canva include:

- **Social media:** Publish or schedule content for Instagram, Facebook, Twitter, LinkedIn, Pinterest, and more.
- **Website:** Design a website and publish it through Canva. You can also use your own domain here.
- **Presentation mode:** Display your design as a live presentation. As a cherry on top, Canva offers options to present and record simultaneously.

- **Embed:** Embed your designs on other websites such as Medium, WordPress, or your own personal blog.
- **Message:** Use Gmail, Whatsapp, iMessage, or Facebook Messenger to send your design as a message.
- **Design:** Open your design with Heyzine Flipbooks or Simplebooklet Flip.
- **Save:** Save your projects to Google Drive, Dropbox, Microsoft OneDrive or as a Microsoft PowerPoint.
- **More options:** Use more options to drop your files from a source and edit them in Canva. These include HubSpot, Gain, PandaDoc, and many more!

Here are the steps you'll need to publish your design on social media:

1. Click "Share" → "More."
2. Select a platform (such as Instagram or Facebook).
3. Log in to your account if prompted.
4. Add a caption or description if needed.
5. Click "Post" or "Publish."

Tip: Canva's Content Planner (Pro feature) allows you to schedule social media posts in advance.

Back to You

And with that, you've just created your first-ever design with Canva! But that's not all – you're just getting started. We've covered the basics, from navigating the interface to adding elements, customizing text, and sharing your design.

Now that you have a solid foundation, it's time to take your skills to the next level. In the next chapters, we'll get deep into the art of design – how to truly ace aesthetics, create visually stunning layouts, and make your designs stand out effortlessly. Get ready to refine your creative eye and bring your ideas to life like a pro!

Colors, Text, and Typography Mastery

Practice design, not decoration: Don't just make pretty talking points. Instead, display information in a way that makes complex information clear. – Nancy Duarte

Have you ever wondered why some designs instantly grab your attention while others get scrolled past without a second glance? The secret is not just in bold colors or trendy fonts – it is visual hierarchy. This concept is the backbone of great design. It guides the viewer's eyes, creates balance, and ensures the message lands exactly how you intend.

Similar to a magazine, where the title grabs your attention first, the tagline pulls you in, and the more minor details seamlessly lead you deeper into the content, visual hierarchy is what makes a design feel effortless and engaging.

Mastering this concept means understanding how to strategically use color, text, and typography. The right color choices can evoke emotion, create contrast, and highlight key elements. Typography sets the tone, enhances readability, and gives your design personality. How you arrange text – its size, weight, spacing, and alignment, can either make your message clear and compelling or get lost in visual noise.

In this chapter, let's break down how to use color to create impact, pick and pair fonts that complement your design, and structure text elements for balance and clarity!

What Is Color Theory?

Color theory is the foundation of design, art, and visual communication. It explains how colors interact, how they influence emotions, and how they can be combined effectively.

Color theory covers a wide range of definitions, concepts, and design applications – enough to fill entire encyclopedias. However, there are three fundamental categories that are both logical and practical: the color wheel, color harmony, and the context in which colors are applied. Here is a detailed look at all three:

The Color Wheel

The color wheel is a circular chart that arranges colors in a spectrum according to how they relate to one another. It's a key tool for understanding color theory and creating balanced, harmonious designs.

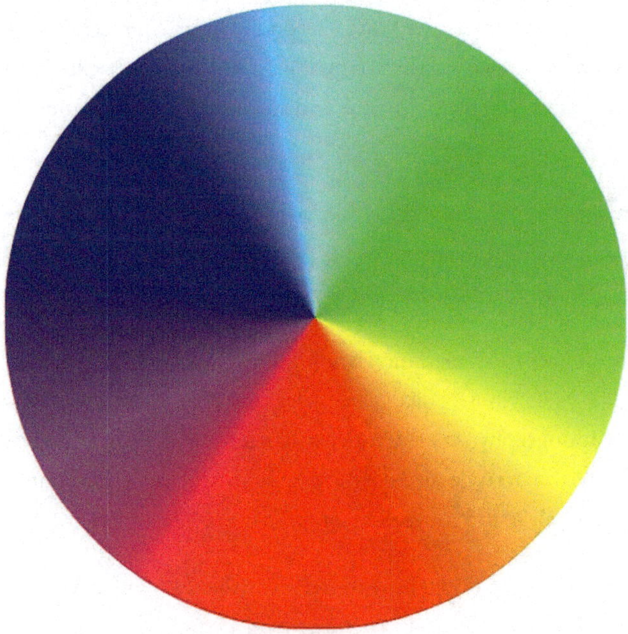

Developed by Sir Isaac Newton in 1666, the color wheel categorizes colors into primary, secondary, and tertiary groups, which helps designers mix, match, and select colors with purpose.

Feature	Examples	Purpose
Primary colors	red, blue, yellow	• the foundation of the color wheel • cannot be created by mixing other colors
Secondary colors	orange (red + yellow), green (blue + yellow), purple (blue + red)	• created by mixing two primary colors • add variety and richness to a color scheme
Tertiary colors	red-orange, yellow-orange, yellow-green, blue-green, blue-purple, red-purple	• created by mixing a primary color with a neighboring secondary color • add depth and complexity
Warm colors	red, orange, yellow	• evoke feelings of energy, passion, and warmth • often used to grab attention
Cool colors	blue, green, purple	• evoke feelings of calm, tranquility, and relaxation • often used for soothing or calming effects
Complementary colors	red and green, blue and orange, yellow and purple	• opposites on the color wheel • when paired together, they create high contrast and vibrancy
Analogous colors	blue, blue-green, green; red, red-orange, orange	• sit next to each other on the color wheel • create harmonious and unified designs
Split-complementary colors	base color: blue complementary colors: red-orange and yellow-orange	• uses one base color and two adjacent colors to its complementary • offers high contrast with less tension

The Color Harmony

Color harmony refers to the use of colors in a design that are visually pleasing and balanced. It's about creating a sense of order and coherence with color combinations that work well together. There are several color schemes used to create harmony, each offering a unique effect or mood:

Monochromatic Color Scheme

- This scheme involves using different shades, tints, and tones of a single color. For example, light blue, medium blue, and dark blue all together.
- Monochromatic schemes are calm, cohesive, and easy on the eyes. They create a sense of simplicity and elegance.
- These schemes are ideal for designs where a minimalist, clean, or professional feel is desired.

Analogous Color Scheme

- This scheme uses colors that sit next to each other on the color wheel, such as blue, blue-green, and green, or red, red-orange, and orange.
- Analogous colors blend harmoniously and create a serene and unified look. The colors naturally complement each other and tend to feel comfortable.
- These schemes are great for designs that want to evoke a calm, peaceful vibe. It's often used in nature-based designs or relaxed settings.

Complementary Color Scheme

- Complementary colors are situated opposite to each other on the color wheel.
- These colors create a bold, high-contrast look that makes the design stand out. When used properly, they can be dynamic and attention-grabbing.
- These schemes are perfect for designs that need boldness or when you want to emphasize a specific element. They are often used in advertising to attract attention.

Split-Complementary Color Scheme

- This color scheme involves a base color and the two colors adjacent to its direct opposite on the color wheel. For instance, with blue as the base, the scheme would include the colors on either side of its complement, such as red-orange or yellow-orange.
- This scheme offers the contrast of complementary colors but with less tension, making it more versatile. It provides a balance of vibrant contrast and harmony.
- These schemes are ideal for designs that want a bit of energy without the intensity of a straight complementary scheme.

Color harmony ensures the colors work together, enhances the overall aesthetic, and makes the design approachable. You need to consider harmony if you want to deliver your intended message and leave an emotional impact on your viewers.

The Context of Colors

When you're choosing colors for your design, context is everything. The same color can feel completely different depending on where and how you use it – so it's essential to think beyond just what looks good.

Start by considering culture. Colors don't have universal meanings. Red might symbolize good luck and celebration in one culture but signal danger or urgency in another. Always keep your audience in mind and do a bit of research if your design is going global.

Think about your brand, too. The colors you choose should match your brand's personality and values. If you want to build trust, blue is a solid choice. Want to show you're eco-friendly or health-conscious? Green does the job. Every color sends a message – make sure it's the right one.

Don't forget about the medium. Colors look different on a screen, on paper, or in a physical product. What looks vibrant on your laptop might print out dull or appear overly bright on a phone. Always test your colors on the platform where your audience will see them.

In functional design, like websites or apps, colors do more than decorate. They guide people. A red button might mean "stop" or "error," while green signals "go" or "success." Use color intentionally to make navigation intuitive and clear.

In the end, color is more than a style choice – it's a communication tool. When you use it with purpose and context in mind, you'll create designs that not only look great but truly connect with your audience.

How Canva Helps With Colors

You'll love Canva for the variety of tools and features it provides you to choose and work with colors effectively. Check and try all of these out for yourself so that you can see which colors work for you and which don't:

Pre-Made Color Palettes

Canva provides a library of pre-designed color palettes that are ready to use. These palettes are curated by design professionals and are grouped by moods, themes, or purposes so you can easily find a harmonious color scheme for your project.

Color Wheel

Canva has a built-in color wheel that allows users to pick colors based on a specific scheme, such as complementary, analogous, or triadic colors. This helps ensure your color choices are visually appealing and balanced without needing a deep understanding of color theory.

Color Picker

Canva offers a color picker tool that lets you select any color from an image or design element within the platform. This feature is helpful when trying to match the colors in your design with specific images or other elements.

Gradient and Transparency Options

Canva allows users to create gradient backgrounds with different colors, helping you craft unique and visually interesting designs. Additionally, you can adjust the transparency of colors and elements to create layers and depth in your design.

Contrast Checker

Canva's contrast tool helps ensure that text and background color combinations meet accessibility standards, improving readability and usability for all users. This tool is especially important for ensuring your designs are visually accessible to a broader audience.

Color Harmony Suggestions

Canva's design suggestions often include color harmony features that automatically suggest colors that complement or contrast each other well and help to create a professional look and feel.

Custom Colors

You can input specific hex codes or RGB values in Canva to use custom colors, ensuring your design aligns with your brand or personal color preferences.

To find hex codes for colors, you can use a color picker tool available in design software like Canva or online tools like Adobe Color, Coolors, or a browser extension.

Simply select the color you want, and the tool will provide the hex code, which is a 6-digit code that represents the color in the RGB spectrum (such as #FF5733, which is a vibrant shade of red). You can also find hex codes in design palettes or by inspecting elements on websites using browser developer tools.

Once you have the hex code, you can input it directly into Canva to use that specific color in your design.

By providing these tools, Canva makes it easier for both beginners and advanced designers to apply color theory and create designs that are visually balanced, harmonious, and effective in conveying their intended message.

Text and Typography in Design

In design, text and typography are often used interchangeably. While text is the written content itself, typography is the art of arranging that text to make it aesthetically appealing, readable, and effective in communicating its intended message. Let's first talk about the text itself:

What Is Text in Design?

Text in design refers to the written words – letters, numbers, symbols – used to convey a message. It's the content itself: the story you're telling, the information you're sharing, or the point you're making. Text can be seen in:

- **Headlines:** the main titles of your design (They grab attention and summarize the most important message.)
- **Body text or paragraphs:** the supporting information that gives depth and context to your headline
- **Captions, footnotes, and annotations:** smaller text that provides additional details; often used to clarify or add context to the main content
- **Call-to-action buttons:** text designed to encourage action, like "Sign Up," "Learn More," or "Buy Now"

When it comes to how much text you should have in a design, *less* is often more but that's not to say you should leave important information out. Here are a few rules to keep in mind:

- Keep the text minimal to communicate the message clearly and respect short attention spans.
- Write punchy headlines with 6–10 words to grab attention without overwhelming the reader.
- Create a visual hierarchy using size and font weight so the most important information stands out first.
- Use bold, italics, or underlining to emphasize key points and create contrast.
- Keep the amount of text balanced with the design's size and purpose to maintain a clean layout.
- Use easy-to-read fonts and keep body text around 14–16 points for better legibility.

- Avoid small or thin fonts in fast-scanning environments like websites or mobile apps.
- Allow for white space to give the design room to breathe and make content easier to digest.
- Make sure every piece of text has a purpose – remove anything that doesn't add value.
- Use strong contrast between text and background to maintain readability.
- If the background is busy, add a semi-transparent overlay to help the text stand out.

The 80/20 Rule

A good guideline for how much text to include in a design is the 80/20 rule. This rule suggests that 80% of your design should be visual elements (such as images, icons, and colors), while only 20% should be text. This ratio keeps your design clean, engaging, and visually appealing, allowing your message to shine through without overwhelming the viewer.

Here is what *not* to do when placing text on your design:

Avoid Overcrowding

It's tempting to fit as much information as possible into one design, but it can quickly become chaotic. Too much text in too little space can make the design look cluttered and unprofessional.

Don't Use Too Many Fonts

Mixing too many different fonts can make a design feel disorganized. Stick to a maximum of two or three fonts – one for headings, one for body text, and one for any additional accents, if necessary.

Steer Clear of Hard-To-Read Fonts

Artistic or decorative fonts can look fun, but if they're hard to read, they defeat the purpose of text. Always prioritize readability over aesthetics when designing for communication.

All in all, keep your text concise, readable, and purpose-driven, and you'll create designs that communicate clearly, engage viewers, and look visually appealing at the same time.

What Is Typography?

Typography is the technique of arranging text in a visually appealing and effective way. It goes beyond simply choosing fonts and involves selecting, sizing, spacing, and aligning text to ensure the design is functional, aesthetically pleasing, and easy to read. Typography helps create a mood, direct attention, and establish hierarchy in design.

The main elements of typography include:

- **Typeface:** This is the font family you choose. Common examples of font families in Canva include Canva Sans, a clean and modern sans-serif font created specifically for the platform; Playfair Display, a classic serif font known for its elegance and sophistication; and Poppins, a geometric sans-serif that's popular for its minimal, contemporary feel.

- **Font weight:** This refers to the thickness of the letters, such as regular, bold, light, or extra bold.

- **Font size:** This is how large or small the text appears. The size of text can be adjusted for emphasis, readability, or to fit the design.

- **Line spacing (leading):** This refers to the space between lines of text. Proper line spacing ensures that the text doesn't feel cramped or too spread out, making it more readable.

- **Letter spacing (tracking):** This is the spacing between letters. Adjusting tracking can affect the overall feel of the text, from tight and compact to open and airy.

- **Alignment:** This refers to the positioning of text on the page – left-aligned, right-aligned, centered, or justified. The alignment helps organize the text and create a balanced layout.
- **Contrast:** This is used to generate visual interest by varying the weight, size, and style of text. For instance, a bold headline adjacent to regular body text draws the reader's attention and emphasizes key details.
- **Hierarchy:** This refers to the organization of text to establish importance. Larger, bolder text can be used for headings, while smaller text can be used for body copy or footnotes.
- **Kerning:** This is the space between individual letters, adjusted for better legibility and visual appeal. For example, in the word "AVOCADO," you might adjust the kerning so the spacing between the "A" and "V" looks visually even.

How Canva Helps With Typography

Canva makes working with typography accessible to everyone, whether you're a beginner or a professional. Here's how Canva can help you use typography effectively in your designs:

Wide Variety of Fonts

Canva provides an extensive library of fonts to choose from, spanning various styles such as serif, sans-serif, script, and display fonts. You can search for fonts by style, making it easy to find the perfect fit for your design's tone.

Font Pairing Suggestions

One of Canva's best features is its font pairing tool. Canva recommends complementary font pairs, which helps ensure that your design looks cohesive. This takes the guesswork out of choosing fonts that work well together, whether you're creating a modern, minimalist design or a more ornate, vintage look.

Adjustable Font Sizes

Canva allows you to adjust font size easily by dragging the text box or entering a specific number. This flexibility helps you create effective visual hierarchies, ensuring the most important information stands out.

Text Effects and Styling

Canva offers many text effects like shadow, outline, lift, and neon, which allow you to enhance the visual impact of your typography. You can also adjust letter spacing (tracking) and line height (leading) directly from the text toolbar.

Text Alignment

With Canva, you can quickly align your text to the left, right, center, or justify it. Proper alignment helps create a polished, professional design, and Canva makes this feature easy to adjust at any time.

Text Colors and Contrast

You can choose from a wide range of colors for your text by selecting from preset options or entering specific hex codes to match your brand's colors. Canva also ensures that your text maintains enough contrast with the background to be readable.

Pre-Made Templates

Canva has a vast selection of templates with pre-arranged text and typography, so you can jump right in and customize it to fit your needs. These templates often include good typography practices, such as balanced font sizes, text alignments, and clear hierarchies, giving you a solid foundation to build on.

Customizable Text Boxes

Canva allows you to adjust the size and shape of text boxes easily. You can resize them to fit your text perfectly or drag the edges to make room for more. This flexibility is great for fitting your text into specific design layouts, like posters, social media posts, or presentations.

Keyboard Shortcuts for Text Editing

If you prefer working quickly, Canva has several keyboard shortcuts for text editing, like changing font size, bolding, italicizing, and aligning text. This can simplify your workflow and speed up design adjustments.

Here are some shortcuts that will help you a lot:

Action	Windows shortcut	Mac shortcut
Bold text	Ctrl + B	Cmd + B
Italicize text	Ctrl + I	Cmd + I
Underline text	Ctrl + U	Cmd + U
Increase font size	Ctrl + Shift + >	Cmd + Shift + >
Decrease font size	Ctrl + Shift + <	Cmd + Shift + <
Align left	Ctrl + Shift + L	Cmd + Shift + L
Align center	Ctrl + Shift + C	Cmd + Shift + C
Align right	Ctrl + Shift + R	Cmd + Shift + R
Undo action	Ctrl + Z	Cmd + Z

Back to You

Now that we've explored the world of color, text, and typography, it's time for you to put your new knowledge into action! Design is all about experimentation, so here's an exercise to get your creativity flowing:

Task: Create a Simple Poster or Social Media Graphic

Objective: Use the principles of color theory, text, and typography to create a visually engaging poster or social media graphic.

- **Choose your purpose:** Decide what your design is meant to communicate. Is it a motivational quote? An event announcement? A product promotion? Your purpose will guide your choices.
- **Pick a color scheme:** Use the color wheel to choose a color scheme for your design. Try using a complementary, analogous, or monochromatic scheme based on your message. Consider how the colors make you feel and how you want the viewer to react.
- **Select your fonts:** Choose two to three fonts that complement each other. For the headline, choose a bold and attention-grabbing font. For the body text, pick a font that is easy to read at smaller sizes.
- **Arrange the text:** Play with text size and alignment to create a clear visual hierarchy. Make the most important part of your message stand out by using larger font sizes or different weights (bold/regular).
- **Keep it balanced:** Take a step back and look at your design. Does it feel balanced? Check for any crowded spaces or areas that might feel too empty. Adjust accordingly for harmony and flow.
- **Choose your final touches:** Add finishing touches like icons, shapes, or illustrations to complement the text, but don't overcrowd the design. Less is more!

Once you've finished your design, take a moment to evaluate it:

- Does it communicate your message clearly?
- Does the color scheme evoke the right emotion?
- Is the typography easy to read and appealing?

This task is a great way to practice the principles we've covered. Don't be afraid to play around and try new things – design is all about experimenting and refining! Ready to dive in? Get creative and have fun with it!

In the next chapter, let's take things up a notch with layers, alignment, and design precision that will help you bring structure and polish to your Canva creations. Let's go!

Layers, Alignments, and Design Precision

Precision refers to the condition, quality, or fact of being exact and accurate. But in design, precision is not measured by accuracy – it is measured by intention, consistency, the alignment of text and images, and the thoughtful arrangement of visual components that convey your message clearly and effectively.

If you think about it, precision influences how viewers perceive your work. A design that lacks precision can feel cluttered, chaotic, or rushed. Misaligned elements, uneven spacing, or improperly layered components can distract from the overall message you're trying to convey. So, let's learn how to use layers, alignment, and design accuracy to achieve the same goals but with precision!

Layer Management

Just like in any other design software, the layers feature in Canva allows you to organize and control the stacking order of elements in your design.

When you add elements such as text, images, shapes, or illustrations, each is placed on its own layer. The layers panel in Canva helps you manage these elements more efficiently and makes it easier to work with multiple components in your design.

Using the layers panel allows for easier editing and modification of individual elements without disrupting the rest of the design. In the past, designers had to dismantle a design to access and move a specific element, only to reassemble everything afterward. With layers, you can adjust each element directly, streamlining your workflow and saving time.

How to Manage Layer Order

To build a logical visual hierarchy and a well-structured design, follow these steps and arrange your layers:

Bring to Front or Send to Back

To rearrange elements in your design, use the "Bring to front" and "Send to back" options. These tools allow you to move an element to the very front or back of the stacking order, ensuring that important elements are not hidden behind others.

Start by right-clicking on your selected element, and then you can adjust the layer accordingly.

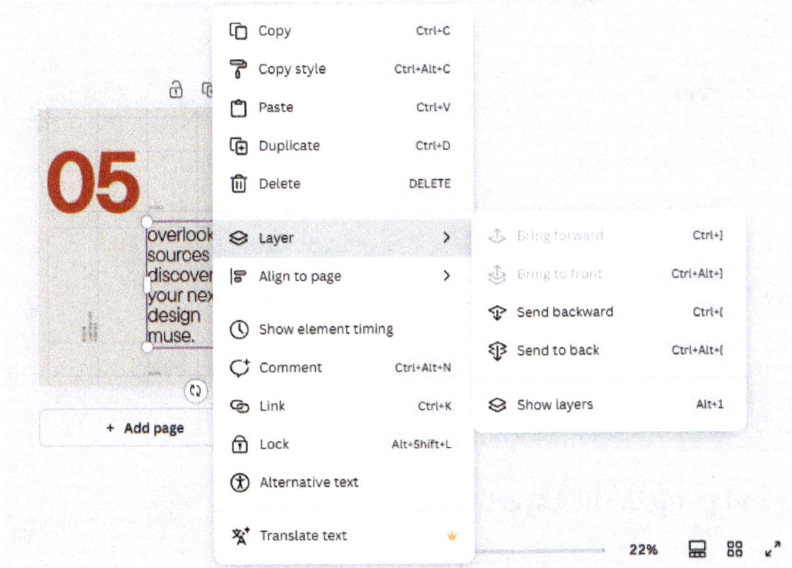

For example, if you have a background image that you want to stay behind your text, simply send the image to the back and keep the text at the front.

Duplicate Layers

To create a copy of a layer, select it and click the "Duplicate" option in the menu or use the keyboard shortcut (Ctrl + D or Cmd + D).

Hide Layers

To temporarily hide a layer, click the eye icon next to it in the layers panel. This allows you to concentrate on specific elements without distractions.

Lock Layers

To prevent unintended or accidental changes, lock a layer by selecting it and clicking the lock icon in the layers panel.

Group Layers

To manage several layers at once, hold Shift while selecting them. Then, right-click and choose "Group" to combine them for easier collective movement or resizing.

Delete Unused Layers

To keep your design clutter-free, delete any unnecessary layers by selecting them and clicking the delete icon.

Drag and Drop in the Layers Panel

For fine-tuned control, the layers panel allows you to drag and drop elements to rearrange their order. This is particularly helpful when you're working with complex designs containing many layers and want to quickly adjust their stacking order.

Why Layer Order Matters

Layer order affects visual hierarchy. This matters in design because it directs where your audience's eyes will travel first. When an element like a logo needs prominence, bring it to the front. Simply dragging layers up or down the list reshuffles their order on your screen.

Let's suppose that you are designing a business card. It is essential to ensure the contact info comes forward so people don't miss it under fancy graphics. This balancing act gives your design depth.

Positioning Tools and How to Use Them

Positioning tools in Canva are every designer's dream come true. You can use them to arrange, align, and place your design elements accurately and aesthetically.

Align Tool

The align tool helps you position elements relative to one another or the overall canvas. Use this tool to top, middle, bottom, left, right, or center align your text, images, or graphics.

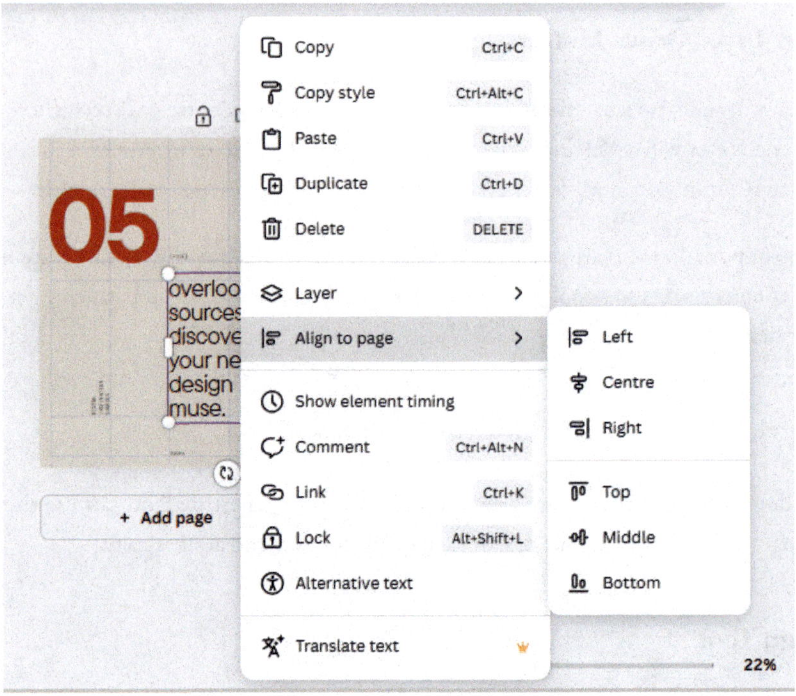

How to Use It

- Select the element you want to align.
- Click on the "Position" button at the top of the Canva Editor.
- Choose one of the alignment options: Top, Middle, Bottom, Left, Center, or Right.
- You can also use the alignment tool to align multiple elements by selecting all of them at once.

Snap to Grid and Ruler in Canva

The grid in Canva provides visual guidance for placing elements on your page, while the ruler offers exact measurements to help maintain consistent spacing.

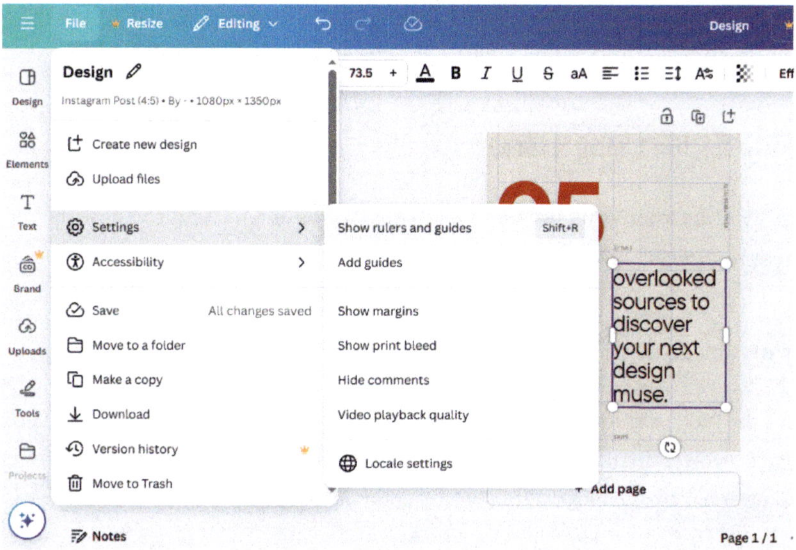

How to Use It

- Access the File menu located at the top of the screen.
- Select "Show ruler" and "Show guides" to activate the ruler and grid on your page. This will display a grid overlay and rulers on the top and left sides of your design area.
- Use the gridlines to help position elements like text boxes, images, and shapes accurately. These gridlines make it easier to line up items perfectly.
- The rulers at the top and left sides of the page show exact measurements. You can drag elements along these rulers to adjust their position.
- You can also adjust the spacing of the gridlines to be closer together or farther apart, depending on your design needs. To do this, go to the File menu and toggle the grid size for finer or broader alignment.

The grid and ruler tools in Canva help create structure and consistency in your designs. When you're working with multiple elements, these tools provide a visual reference to maintain order and alignment and make the design process smoother and more efficient.

These tools can make a big difference in the final outcome, especially in designs like brochures, flyers, or infographics, where spacing and alignment are crucial.

Techniques for Using a Grid

There are some interesting ways to use a grid, and you might want to know them to get different results each time! Let's explore them:

Rely on the Rule of Thirds

One of the most commonly used grid principles, and my personal favorite, is the rule of thirds. It involves dividing your design space, either mentally or using the grid function, into nine equal areas using two horizontal and two vertical lines.

The principle states that placing key compositional elements along these lines or at their intersections (often called "power points" or "sweet spots") creates more balanced, engaging, and visually interesting compositions than simply centering the subject.

For example, in a flyer, you might place your headline along the top horizontal line, with key visuals aligned at the intersections of the vertical and horizontal lines. This draws the viewer's attention in a natural, flowing way.

Try a Modular Grid

A modular grid divides the page into a series of columns and rows, creating a grid that can help you arrange elements in a clear, consistent manner. This is particularly helpful for layouts that require structure, such as magazine pages or websites. By following a modular grid, you can ensure that your content is organized into neat, readable sections.

Maintain Consistent Margins

Grids help maintain equal margins around the edge of your design, improving your layout's visual flow and balance. Consistent margins help guide the viewer's eye into the design rather than letting elements feel like they are "floating" or cramped against the edges.

Avoid Overcrowding

While grids are excellent for organization, it's important not to overcrowd your design with too many elements. Keep your layout clean and simple, with ample white space around your elements to ensure that each part of the design has room to breathe. Grids can help you ensure even spacing, but you should still strive for balance and clarity in your design.

Adjust Grid Opacity

Sometimes, you may want the gridlines to be less prominent so they don't distract from your work. You can adjust the opacity of the grid in Canva's settings and make it lighter or darker, depending on your preference.

Use Temporary Grids for Complex Designs

For more intricate designs, such as multi-page presentations or custom illustrations, you can temporarily add extra guides and grids to help maintain alignment as you work. These guides can be dragged out from the rulers and placed anywhere on the page.

Spacing Tool

Canva also allows you to adjust the spacing between text and other elements within your design. This tool is especially helpful to achieve proper readability and balance.

How to Use It

- Select the text box or element you want to adjust.
- Click on the "Spacing" option in the top toolbar.
- Adjust the letter spacing or line height to achieve the desired look.

Proper spacing between elements makes your design easier to read and visually appealing. Adjusting spacing can prevent text from looking cramped or disorganized.

Centering Tool

If you want to center an element on your page or relative to other elements, Canva offers a quick centering tool that aligns your selection perfectly.

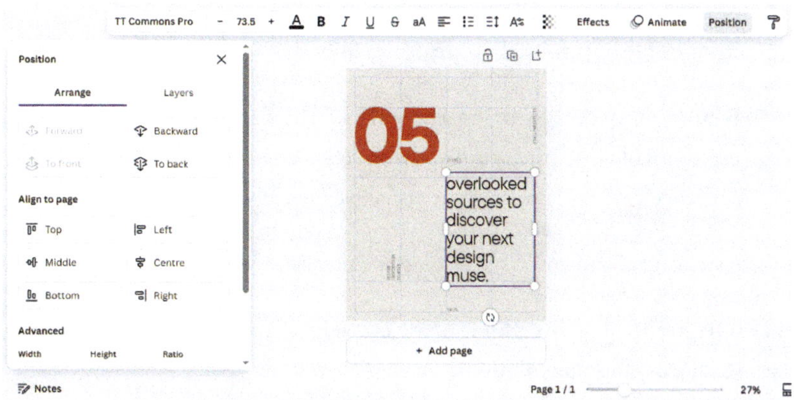

How to Use It

- Select the element you want to center.
- Click on the "Position" button and choose either "Center" for horizontal centering or "Middle" for vertical centering.

This tool helps you quickly center your design components, ensuring a balanced and neat layout. It's especially useful for creating focal points in your design or aligning key elements symmetrically.

It may take a bit of practice to master these tools, but trust me, once you get the hang of them, you'll never look back!

Back to You

Do you want your designs to feel organized, balanced, and visually appealing? You can achieve just that with the layer management and positioning and alignment tools. Ready to refine your design skills? Here is what you can do next:

1. **Practice using the alignment tools:** Choose a project and focus on aligning all elements (text, images, and shapes) using Canva's alignment features, including the grid and ruler tools.
2. **Experiment with layer order:** Try layering different elements and adjust their

order to see how it affects the flow of your design. Bring key elements to the front or push them back to create depth.

3. **Refine your design using the rule of thirds:** Set up a grid in Canva and use the Rule of Thirds to place your key elements. This will help guide your audience's eye and improve the visual balance of your design.

Take these steps now, and you'll start seeing the precision in your work come to life!

The next chapter is all about adding some movement and magic to your designs with animations, videos, and presentations!

Animations, Videos, and Presentations

In our digital world, video content is king. Brands, influencers, and businesses are shifting away from text-based content and static images to dynamic videos and animations to capture their audiences. According to a 2023 report by Wyzowl, 89% of consumers said they were persuaded to buy a product or service *after* watching a brand's video.

Why? Because videos and animations are more engaging, memorable, and shareable. Viewers retain information better from videos compared to text alone, which makes them a powerful tool for communication. Animated content also helps brands stand out in crowded feeds.

Creating video-based content is quite a hassle, but do not worry! Canva makes it easy for anyone to create stunning animations, videos, and presentations – without having to learn Final Cut Pro or DaVinci Resolve.

In this chapter, let's learn the best practices to add motion to your designs, create simple but impactful videos, and create engaging presentations that inspire and captivate your audience.

Creating Videos on Canva

If video is your go-to medium, you are in good company. Canva users have embraced video creation in a big way, with 480 million videos published in 2021 alone. This surge in video content was not a surprise because Canva makes it incredibly easy to create professional-looking videos without the need for advanced editing skills.

Here are some reasons why Canva is an excellent choice for video creation:

- **Scene-based editor:** Canva takes a slide-based approach to video editing, so if you are familiar with creating presentations, you'll find the learning curve almost nonexistent. If you are unfamiliar with creating presentations, we'll discuss that in detail later on, so you are all set either way!
- **Single layer timeline on desktop and mobile:** The timeline editor lets users effortlessly rearrange, extend, or split scenes. Smooth cinematic transitions result in seamless storytelling, and since Canva is optimized for browsers and mobile devices, there is no need for high-end hardware.
- **Multiple audio tracks:** You can layer multiple audio tracks in the video timeline, whether uploading your own files or choosing from Canva's media library. Canva Pro subscribers also get access to 27,000 royalty-free tracks through Epidemic Sound, with thousands of sound effects added.
- **Screen and camera recording:** Canva now allows users to record video from their screen, camera, or Chrome tab, which makes it perfect for tutorials, video messages, or presentations.

Steps to Create a Video Design in Canva

You are just a few steps away from creating a professional-looking video in Canva. Here is how:

Step 1: Start a New Video Project

1. Open Canva and click on the "Create a design" button.
2. In the search bar at the top of the drop-down menu, type "video."
3. Select a video format that best fits your needs (for example, landscape, square, or vertical).
4. The Canva Editor will open and display a blank canvas along with a left-side panel containing various tools and templates.

Step 2: Choose a Video Template

1. Click on the Templates tab in the left sidebar.
2. Browse through the extensive collection of video templates or use the search bar to find a design that aligns with your vision (for instance, type "portfolio" for a professional look).
3. Click on a template to apply it to your design. You can customize it later to fit your style.

Step 3: Add Video Clips to Your Design

You can add videos to your design in two ways.

To upload existing video files:

1. Click on the Uploads tab in the left sidebar.
2. Click "Upload files" to add video clips from your computer, phone, or cloud storage.
3. Once uploaded, drag and drop the video onto your page.

To record a video directly in Canva:

1. Click the "Record yourself" button.
2. Choose between camera recording (to film yourself), screen recording (to capture your screen), or both.
3. Follow the on-screen prompts to start recording.
4. Once finished, your recorded video will automatically appear in your Uploads folder.

Step 4: Arrange and Edit Your Video

1. Drag and drop your video clips onto the page and resize or reposition them as needed.
2. Use Canva's scene-based timeline to rearrange clips, trim footage, or adjust durations for smooth storytelling.
3. Add cinematic transitions to create a seamless flow between scenes.
4. Enhance your video with text overlays, stickers, animations, and effects to make it more engaging.
5. Adjust the audio by adding background music, sound effects, or narration.

Step 5: Keep It Engaging and Professional

- Use high-quality video clips that match your brand's aesthetic.
- Keep your video concise – ideally under one minute, to maintain viewer interest.
- Make sure that your message is clear, whether you're creating a social media ad, tutorial, or personal project.

Once you're happy with your design, export your video in the best format for your needs. Canva allows you to export videos in the following formats:

- **MP4:** This is the most common format for video files and is suitable for most platforms and devices.
- **GIF:** You can also export simple animated videos as GIF files.

Now, you're ready to share your creation with the world!

What Is Magic Design and How Can You Use It?

Magic Design is a feature in Canva that uses artificial intelligence to help you generate design layouts and templates quickly and easily. It allows you to input specific elements or ideas, and the tool will automatically create design options based on your input. The best part is that you can even modify and personalize the suggested designs by changing colors, fonts, images, and other elements.

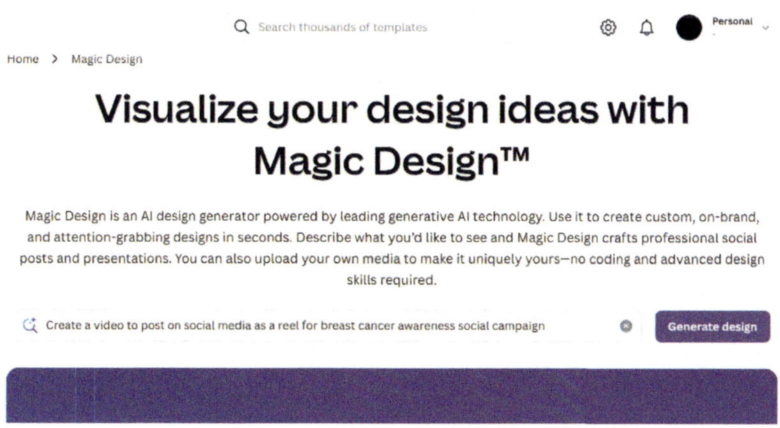

To create a video using Magic Design, follow these steps:

1. Type in the URL canva.com/magic-design/ or search Canva Magic Design on the web and click on the Magic Design tool.
2. Enter a brief description of your video concept (preferably in more than five words) to help Canva understand your idea.
3. Click "Generate" to create your video instantly

Limitations

Magic Design is a great feature, but it comes with some considerations.

- The videos created by Magic Design work with social media formats like Instagram Reels and TikTok, as well as standard video formats (1920 × 1080px horizontal, 1080 × 1920px vertical, or 1080 ×x 1920px square). While videos can be any size, extremely large or small videos may affect the final quality.
- When uploading to YouTube, make sure you're signed into the account connected to Canva to prevent content claims.

- The outcome depends on how much information and detail you provide.

Getting Started With Animations

Adding animations to your designs is a great way to bring them to life and grab your audience's attention. Animations can highlight key elements, guide the viewer's eye, and create a more dynamic, engaging experience. However, using them thoughtfully is essential, too many animations can distract from your message, so it's best to animate only the most important elements.

Here is how to add animations to your designs in Canva:

1. **Open your design:** Start by opening your portfolio or any other project in Canva's editor.
2. **Select an element:** Click on any element you want to animate, such as an image or a text box.
3. **Choose your animation:** In the top toolbar, click on the "Animate" button. If it is not visible, click the three dots on the right side of the toolbar to reveal it. You will see a list of animation options like Fade, Pan, Pop, and Rise.
4. **Explore and customize:** Scroll through the different animation styles in the left sidebar and experiment with them. You can adjust animation settings, such as when the effect happens (on enter, on exit, or both), and control the speed of the animation.
5. **Fine-tune your animation**: Use the sliders and buttons to tweak the settings to your liking. For example, you can make the animation slower or faster or choose when it appears.
6. **Create custom animations**: If you want to go beyond the preset options, you can click "Animation" under the Tool section in your Animations sidebar to design your own unique animations.

Magic Animate

Magic Animate is a game-changer when it comes to adding dynamic animations and transitions to your design in a flash. What once took hours of manual adjustments is now done in seconds. Using AI, Magic Animate analyzes your design and considers elements like content, font choices, images, and colors to select the most fitting animations and transitions.

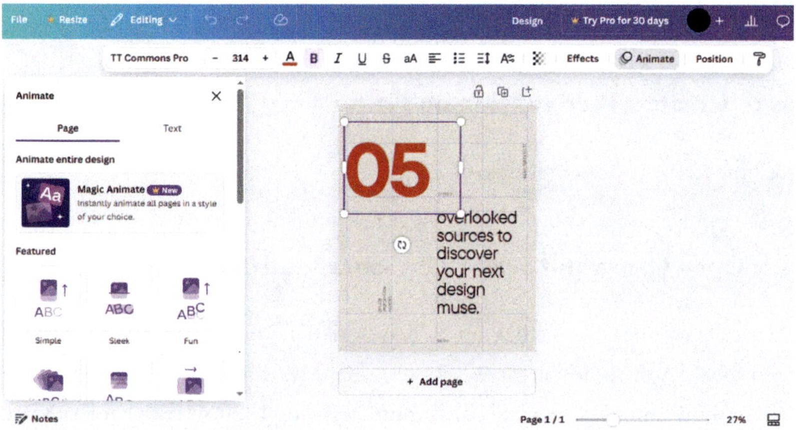

Follow these steps to use Magic Animate:

1. Click on the element you'd like to animate in your design.
2. A bar will appear at the top of your page. Select "Animate."
3. On the left sidebar, click on "Page" and then "Magic Animate" to let Canva work its magic!

And that's it! Your animated GIF or MP4 is ready for use across social media, websites, email, and any platform that supports these formats. Animations are a fun way to elevate your designs, but always aim for balance and simplicity to maintain clarity and impact.

Engaging Presentation Creation

Your presentation deck can help you close a deal, impress stakeholders, leave your classmates in awe, or simply communicate your ideas with clarity and impact. A well-designed presentation not only conveys your message but also keeps your audience engaged and motivated to take action.

Fortunately, with Canva, you can create visually stunning slides that support your storytelling and boost your confidence in any setting.

Steps to Create a Presentation on Canva

Here is how to create presentations on Canva:

Step 1: Open Canva and Select a Presentation Format

On the homepage of Canva, click on "Create a design" button at the top right of the screen. From the drop-down menu, choose the "Presentation" option. Canva offers several pre-sized templates, with the most common being 1920 × 1080px for a widescreen format of 16:9.

Step 2: Choose a Template or Start From Scratch

Canva provides an extensive library of presentation templates that can suit a wide range of styles and themes. You can also search for specific presentation templates, such as "business presentation" or "education presentation," to find the right starting point.

On the left-hand sidebar, browse the various categories or use the search bar to find templates that fit your topic. If you prefer a more customized design, you can choose a blank page and create your presentation slides from scratch.

Step 3: Customize Your First Slide

Once you've selected a template or blank presentation, you can begin customizing the first slide. Canva gives you complete control over text, fonts, images, and design elements.

Click on the text boxes to edit the title and content of your slide. Use the top toolbar to adjust font styles, sizes, and colors, or explore the left sidebar for additional elements like shapes, icons, and illustrations.

Step 4: Add More Slides

To add a new slide, click on the "+" button next to the slide panel on the left or simply press Ctrl + D on Windows or Cmd + D on Mac. You can select different layouts for each slide, depending on your content. A title slide might have a large header, while subsequent slides could be used for bullet points, images, graphs, or quotes.

Step 5: Incorporate Visuals

A presentation with visuals is far more engaging than one filled with just text. Canva lets you easily add high-quality photos, icons, and illustrations.

- To insert an image, click on the Photos tab in the left sidebar, search for an image, and drag it onto the slide.
- You can resize and adjust the placement of the image to suit your design.
- You can also upload your own images by clicking the Uploads tab and selecting "Upload files."

Step 6: Use Animations and Transitions

Follow the steps in the previous section to add animations to your project. For transitions between slides, here's how you can make your presentation flow seamlessly:

1. Click on the slide in the editor that you want to add a transition to.
2. On the top toolbar, click on the "Transition" button. This will open the transition options.
3. Browse through the different transition styles available, such as Fade, Slide, Wipe, Circle, and others. Each transition adds a unique effect to how your slides move from one to the next.

4. After selecting a transition, click on it to apply it to the current slide. You can preview the effect by clicking the "Play" button.
5. Adjust the duration of the transition by moving the slider to the left or right. A shorter duration gives a quicker, more dynamic change between slides, while a longer one adds a more dramatic effect.
6. If you want to apply the same transition to multiple slides, simply click on the "Apply to all" button. This ensures that each slide has the same transition effect.
7. Once the transitions are set, click the "Play" button at the top of the screen to preview how the slides will transition during your presentation. You can adjust transitions or durations if necessary.

Step 7: Edit and Format for Clarity

As you design, always make sure the text is legible and the slides are not cluttered. Leave ample space between elements, and ensure the font size is large enough for readability. Canva provides alignment tools (visible when you move elements around) that help ensure everything is neatly aligned. If you're presenting on a large screen, make sure your font sizes and images are scalable to ensure visibility.

Step 8: Collaborate With Team Members

Canva's collaboration feature allows you to work together with others on your presentation in real time. Click the "Share" button in the top right corner of the editor, and you can invite team members to view or edit the presentation. This feature is especially useful for group projects or when you want feedback from a colleague or client before finalizing the design.

Step 9: Export and Present

Once your presentation is complete, it's time to export it. Canva offers several download options depending on your needs. You can export your presentation as a high-quality PDF, PNG, or JPG, or you can choose to download it as a video file (MP4) if you've included animations and audio. To start the export process, click on the "Download" button in the top-right corner and select the desired format.

By following these steps, you'll be able to create a visually engaging and professional presentation that will leave a lasting impression on your audience.

Bonus: Using ChatGPT with Canva
You can now integrate Canva with ChatGPT to easily discover and generate templates. This feature is in its Beta stage and is exclusively available to ChatGPT Plus users and developers.
To get started:

1. Log in to your ChatGPT Plus account.
2. Go to "Explore GPTs" and search for Canva. This will activate the Canva plugin.
3. In the message field, describe your design needs in detail, including the style and elements you're looking for.

ChatGPT will help you find the perfect Canva template for your presentation based on your description.

Back to You

Now that you've learned the ins and outs of creating videos, animations, and presentations, it's time to take action! Here are three steps you can take right now:

1. **Choose your video concept:** Think of a concept for a short video, whether it's a promotional video, a personal message, or a tutorial. Define the purpose and message you want to convey clearly.

2. **Find a relevant template:** Head to Canva and search for a video template that aligns with your concept. There are plenty of options available that can be customized to suit your style and needs. Choose one that works best for your vision.

3. **Edit and export your video:** Customize the template by adding your own text, images, and videos. Play with animations, transitions, and music to enhance your content. Once you're satisfied with your design, export the video in the

desired format and get ready to share it!

Start experimenting today, and watch your video come to life!

Next up, we will talk about creating social media graphics, where you will learn how to design eye-catching visuals that captivate your audience and boost your online presence!

Crafting Social Media Graphics With Canva

Do you remember Apple's "Shot on iPhone" campaign? It is a perfect example of how powerful images can tell a brand story. With minimal text and stunning visuals, Apple showcases the capabilities of its iPhone camera by featuring breathtaking images captured by everyday users. This campaign was successful because it tapped into the idea that anyone could create professional-quality content, aligning with Apple's message of empowering individuals through technology.

You can apply the same concept to your brand using Canva. You don't need a big marketing budget or a professional design team to create visually compelling content that tells your story. With Canva's intuitive design tools, customizable templates, and vast media library, you can create eye-catching graphics, engaging social media posts, and polished branding materials that capture your audience's attention.

In this chapter, we'll explore how to use Canva to build a strong visual presence for your brand. Are you ready to go from zero to a hundred thousand followers organically?

Step 1: Creating a Cohesive Visual Identity

What's the first thing people notice when they come across your brand online? The colors, fonts, and design elements you use. These elements create your brand's visual identity and play a crucial role in how your audience perceives you. A strong, recognizable brand presence helps build trust and credibility, whether you're an entrepreneur, small business owner, or content creator.

Choosing the Right Colors, Fonts, and Design Elements

Your brand's visual identity should align with your message, values, and audience. Here's how to make the right choices:

- **Colors:** Different colors evoke different emotions. For example, blue conveys trust and professionalism, while red is bold and energetic. Canva's color palette generator can help you find the perfect shades that align with your brand's personality.

- **Fonts:** Typography affects readability and tone. Serif fonts feel classic and professional, while sans-serif fonts are modern and minimalistic. Canva provides font pairing suggestions to help you maintain a balanced look.

- **Design Elements:** Icons, patterns, and shapes can reinforce your brand's message. Keep them consistent to create a visually harmonious aesthetic.

Creating a Brand Kit in Canva

With its Brand Kit feature, Canva makes it easy to maintain consistency across all your designs. It is available only in the Pro version but absolutely worth it! Here's what you can do:

- **Upload your logo:** Store multiple versions of your logo to use across different designs.

- **Set your color palette:** Save your brand colors so they're easily accessible in every project.

- **Choose your fonts:** Select your primary and secondary fonts to keep your branding uniform across graphics.

Once your Brand Kit is set up, Canva allows you to apply it to templates effortlessly. This way, you won't have to upload it every time you start working on a design!

The Importance of Consistency Across Social Media

Your social media visuals should be instantly recognizable to your audience. Whether someone sees your Instagram post, X (formerly Twitter) banner, or YouTube thumbnail, they should immediately associate it with your brand. To achieve this

- stick to your brand colors and fonts in all your designs.
- use the same filters and editing styles for your images.
- keep a uniform tone and style in your captions and messaging.

Step 2: Defining Your Social Media Strategy

With a solid brand identity in place, the next step is to plan your posts and their purpose. A well-crafted strategy ensures your social media efforts are in sync with your business goals and helps you engage with the right audience.

Understanding Your Target Audience

Before creating content, take a step back and analyze who you are trying to reach. Understanding your audience's behaviors, preferences, and challenges will allow you to craft content that speaks directly to them.

Ask yourself these questions:

- *Who am I trying to reach?* (demographics such as age, interests, challenges, and buying behaviors)
- *Where do they spend their time online?* (Instagram, LinkedIn, TikTok, Facebook, Pinterest, and so on)
- *What type of content resonates with them?* (inspirational, educational, entertaining, informative, behind-the-scenes)

Here are some examples:

- If your target audience is Gen Z and millennials, they are likely active on Instagram, TikTok, and YouTube, where short-form videos and visually engaging content work best.
- If you're targeting business professionals, LinkedIn and X are better suited for thought leadership content and industry discussions.
- If you're in the DIY, lifestyle, or food niche, Pinterest is an excellent platform for driving traffic to your blog or website.

Setting Clear Goals: Engagement, Reach, or Conversions?

Not all social media posts serve the same purpose. Some are designed to engage your existing audience, some to expand your reach, and others to convert followers into customers. Defining your goals will help you create the right type of content.

- For engagement, such as likes, comments, and shares, create interactive posts like polls, quizzes, and Q&A sessions to encourage conversations. Use eye-catching carousel posts, GIFs, and memes to make your brand more relatable.
- For reach, use bold, scroll-stopping visuals, trending hashtags, and shareable infographics. Design high-quality quote graphics or educational posts that encourage people to save and share them.
- For conversion, design persuasive product images, testimonials, and promotional banners with strong call-to-action elements like "Shop now," "Sign up," or "Download." Use Canva to create branded sales graphics and product mockups that stand out.

Canva makes it easy to design content for each goal with templates that match different objectives. All you need to do is search for the right keyword and you'll see a great variety to choose from!

Creating a Content Calendar and Planning Posts Ahead of Time

One of the biggest challenges of social media is consistency. Plan your content in advance instead of scrambling to create posts daily. Having a content calendar will help you stay organized and post regularly without feeling overwhelmed.

Here's how to plan your content efficiently:

- **Use Canva's content planner:** Canva Pro users can schedule and publish posts directly from Canva, making it easy to streamline their workflow.
- **Batch-create graphics:** Instead of designing one post at a time, create multiple posts in one sitting. Design a week's worth of Instagram posts or an entire month's worth of Pinterest graphics in one session.
- **Repurpose content:** A single piece of content can be transformed into multiple formats:
    - A blog post can be turned into an infographic, quote graphic, and Instagram story.
    - A video snippet from a podcast can be turned into a short-form video for TikTok and Reels.
- **Plan around key events and trends:** Identify upcoming holidays, product launches, or industry trends and create branded seasonal content ahead of time. Canva provides holiday-themed templates and trending design ideas to help you stay relevant.

With the help of a structured content calendar, you'll stay ahead of the game, maintain a steady flow of high-quality posts, and ensure that your content aligns with your brand's overall marketing goals.

Designing Social Media Posts With Canva

Creating visually appealing and engaging social media posts doesn't have to be time-consuming or complicated. With Canva's premade templates, you can easily design professional-quality graphics that fit your brand and message. Whether you're posting on Instagram, Facebook, X, LinkedIn, Pinterest, or TikTok, Canva has the perfect template.

Using Canva Templates for Social Media

By now, we know that Canva offers thousands of ready-to-use templates designed specifically for different social media platforms. Instead of starting from scratch, you can choose a template that fits your needs and customize it to reflect your brand.

Finding the Right Template

1. Go to Canva and search for the type of post you need. For example: "Instagram post," "Facebook ad," or "Pinterest pin."

2. Browse the available templates and choose one that fits your style and message.

3. Click on the template to open it in the Canva editor.

Platform-Specific Templates Available in Canva

Social media platform	Available templates in Canva
Instagram	posts, stories, reel covers, carousel graphics
Facebook	cover photos, posts, event banners, ads
X	images, headers, engagement posts
Linkedin	company banners, post graphics, article covers
Pinterest	vertical pins, infographics, promotional pins
YouTube	thumbnails, channel banners, video backgrounds
TikTok	video backgrounds, thumbnail templates

Adjusting Image Size for Different Social Media Platforms

One of the most vital aspects of designing social media posts is ensuring they are the correct size for each platform. Canva simplifies this process by allowing you to resize designs instantly.

Standard Social Media Image Sizes

- **Instagram post:** 1080 × 1080 px (square)
- **Instagram story and reel cover:** 1080 × 1920 px (vertical)
- **Facebook post:** 1200 × 630 px
- **Facebook cover photo:** 1640 × 924 px
- **X post:** 1600 × 900 px
- **LinkedIn post:** 1200 × 627 px
- **LinkedIn banner:** 1584 × 396 px
- **Pinterest pin:** 1000 × 1500 px
- **YouTube thumbnail:** 1280 × 720 px
- **TikTok video cover:** 1080 × 1920 px

How to Resize Your Design in Canva

1. Click on "Resize" (Canva Pro feature) in the top menu.
2. Select the desired dimensions from Canva's preset social media sizes.
3. Click "Copy and resize" to create a new version without affecting the original.
4. Adjust the elements and text positioning as needed.

If you don't have Canva Pro, manually adjust the size by

- clicking "Create a new design" and selecting the correct dimensions.
- copying elements from your original design and pasting them into the new size.
- adjusting fonts, images, and layout to fit the new aspect ratio.

For example, if you designed an Instagram post but also want to use it for Pinterest, simply resize it to 1000 × 1500 px and adjust the layout to fit the vertical format.

Designing Ads for Social Media

Social media ads are a powerful tool for reaching your target audience, driving traffic, and increasing conversions. But with so many brands competing for attention, how do you make your ads stand out? The key lies in eye-catching visuals, compelling messaging, and strategic design.

Let's talk about the dos and don'ts of social media advertising and how to use Canva to craft ads that convert.

Do: Keep It Simple and Clear

Your audience is scrolling quickly, so your ad needs to communicate its message at a glance. Use concise text, bold headlines, and strong visuals to make an impact.

For example, instead of "Check out our new collection of sustainable, handcrafted, and ethically sourced shoes," try "Sustainable shoes, made for you."

Don't: Overcrowd Your Design

Too much text, too many colors, and excessive graphics can overwhelm viewers. Keep it clean, balanced, and visually appealing.

Do: Use High-Quality Images and Videos

Blurry or pixelated images make your ad look unprofessional. Canva provides millions of high-resolution stock images and videos, or you can upload your own.

Pro tip: For product ads, showcase your product in real-life scenarios rather than plain backgrounds – it makes the ad more relatable!

Don't: Ignore Aspect Ratios

Different social media platforms have different ad sizes. A design that looks perfect on Instagram Stories might get cropped awkwardly on Facebook.

Solution: Use Canva's preset ad templates to be sure your visuals fit the correct dimensions for each platform.

Do: Include a Strong Call-To-Action (CTA)

Every ad should tell viewers what to do next, whether it's to "Shop now," "Sign up," or "Learn more." Make sure your CTA is

- short and action-oriented.
- easy to find.
- aligned with your goal.

Don't: Use Weak CTAs

Avoid vague phrases like "Click here" or "Check this out." Instead, use action-driven CTAs like:

- "Get yours today!"
- "Claim your free trial!"
- "Start your journey now!"

Automation and Consistency in Posting

Building a strong social media presence requires more than great content – it demands consistency. But let's be honest: Manually creating and posting content every day can be overwhelming.

That's where automation comes in. With tools like Canva's scheduling feature, you can plan, design, and schedule posts ahead of time, freeing you to focus on other aspects of your business. Additionally, creating reusable templates allows you to maintain a cohesive look and feel without reinventing the wheel for every post.

Scheduling Posts With Canva

Canva's built-in Content Planner (available with Canva Pro) allows you to schedule posts across multiple social media platforms directly from Canva. Instead of downloading designs and manually uploading them to each platform, you can set everything up in one place and let Canva handle the rest.

To start scheduling, simply create your design, click the "Share" button, and select "Schedule." From there, choose your preferred platform and set the date and time. Canva will post your content automatically. This feature is especially useful if you're managing multiple accounts or planning content in advance for product launches, seasonal campaigns, or weekly promotions.

Creating Templates for Repeated Use

Creating reusable templates can save you hours of design work if you frequently post similar types of content – such as motivational quotes, promotional offers, or weekly tips. Instead of starting from scratch every time, you can quickly update the text, swap out images, and adjust colors while keeping the overall design intact.

Canva allows you to create and save branded templates that align with your company's aesthetic. All your posts can maintain a consistent look through an organized template library. This is particularly useful for businesses that post on a regular schedule, such as "Motivation Monday" quotes, "Feature Friday" customer stories, or "Tuesday tips" educational posts.

To create a reusable template, design your post once and save it in a dedicated brand folder within Canva. The next time you need a similar post, simply duplicate the design, update the content, and schedule it with minimal effort. This method not only saves time but also reinforces brand identity and makes your feed look polished and professional.

With a combination of automation and templated designs, you can become successful in establishing a social media presence that is both efficient and visually cohesive.

Tracking Campaign Success With Canva Analytics

Once your social media or marketing campaign is live, the final step is evaluating its performance. Tracking your results helps you understand what's working, what isn't, and how you can improve future content.

Canva's Analytics tool offers valuable insights into how your designs perform across various platforms. This will enable you to make data-driven decisions and fine-tune your marketing strategy.

With Canva Analytics, you can monitor how your designs are performing. Instead of guessing which visuals are engaging your audience, you get real-time data that helps you measure impact and optimize your approach.

Why Use Canva Analytics?

Here are some benefits of using Canva Analytics:

Monitor Engagement and Reach

Canva Analytics allows you to track the performance of your designs across multiple channels. Whether it's a social media post, a promotional email, or a digital ad, you can see how many people viewed, interacted with, or engaged with your content. This helps you identify high-performing posts and replicate their success in future campaigns.

Track Essential Metrics

Data-driven marketing is all about measuring the correct numbers. Canva Analytics provides key performance indicators (KPIs) such as:

- **Views:** How many people have seen your design?
- **Clicks:** How often did users take action (such as clicking a link or call-to-action

button)?

- **Engagement rate:** What was the level of interaction, including likes, comments, and shares?

Refine and Improve Future Campaigns

Once you've gathered performance insights, you can make informed adjustments to improve your next campaign. If a particular design or post underperforms, consider tweaking the visuals, adjusting the copy, or experimenting with different layouts. If a post performs exceptionally well, use its design as a template for future content to maintain engagement.

Canva also makes A/B testing easier. You can create multiple versions of a design and test different headlines, colors, or images to see which one generates better results. Over time, this helps you develop a more effective and data-backed marketing strategy.

With all these amazing features at your disposal, there's nothing stopping you from succeeding in the social media landscape!

Back to You

You've got the tools, the knowledge, and the creativity – now it's time to make your social media presence shine! Ready to take action? Here are three powerful steps you can take right now to start leveling up your brand with Canva:

1. Open Canva, choose a template that fits your brand, and customize it with your message, images, and colors. Don't overthink it – just create and post!
2. Build a brand kit inside Canva by selecting your logo, colors, and fonts. Apply these elements consistently across all your designs to make your brand instantly recognizable.
3. Plan ahead! Use Canva's Content Planner (or your own scheduling tool) to organize your upcoming posts and ensure you're showing up consistently.

The more you practice, the easier it will become. Soon, designing eye-catching social media content will feel like second nature. So, go ahead, start creating, experimenting, and watching your brand come to life!

In our next and final chapter, let's explore some of the most frequently asked questions to help you gain further control over your design skills!

Frequently Asked Questions About Canva

Now that you are exploring Canva, chances are you will run into a few questions along the way. In this chapter, we'll tackle the most frequently asked questions about Canva to make your experience even smoother. Let's get to it!

How to Add a Textbox in Canva

Adding a text box in Canva is simple and allows you to customize your design with text elements. Here is how to do it:

Method 1: Using the Text Tool

1. Open your Canva design.
2. Click on the "Text" tab in the left-hand menu.
3. Choose from "Add a heading," "Add a subheading," or "Add a body of text" to insert a text box.
4. Click on the selected option, and a text box will appear on your design.
5. Type your text and customize it using the toolbar at the top (change font, size, color, or alignment).

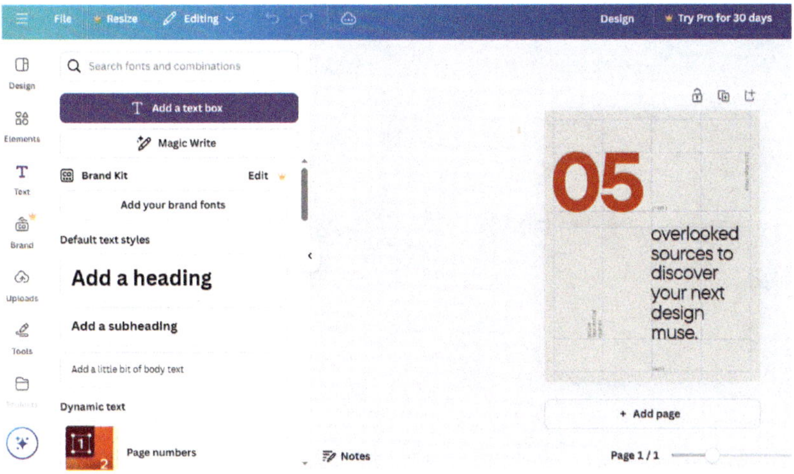

Method 2: Shortcut Method

1. Simply press "T" on your keyboard.

2. A text box will instantly appear on your design.

Adding text in Canva is effortless, and with a few clicks, you can create stylish, professional-looking typography for your designs!

How to Upload Fonts to Canva

If you are using Canva Pro, Canva for Teams, Canva for Education, or Canva for Nonprofits, you can upload custom fonts to match your brand's style. Here is how:

Step 1: Access the Brand Kit

1. Open Canva and go to the Home page.

2. Click on "Brand" in the left-side menu.

3. Select "Brand Kit."

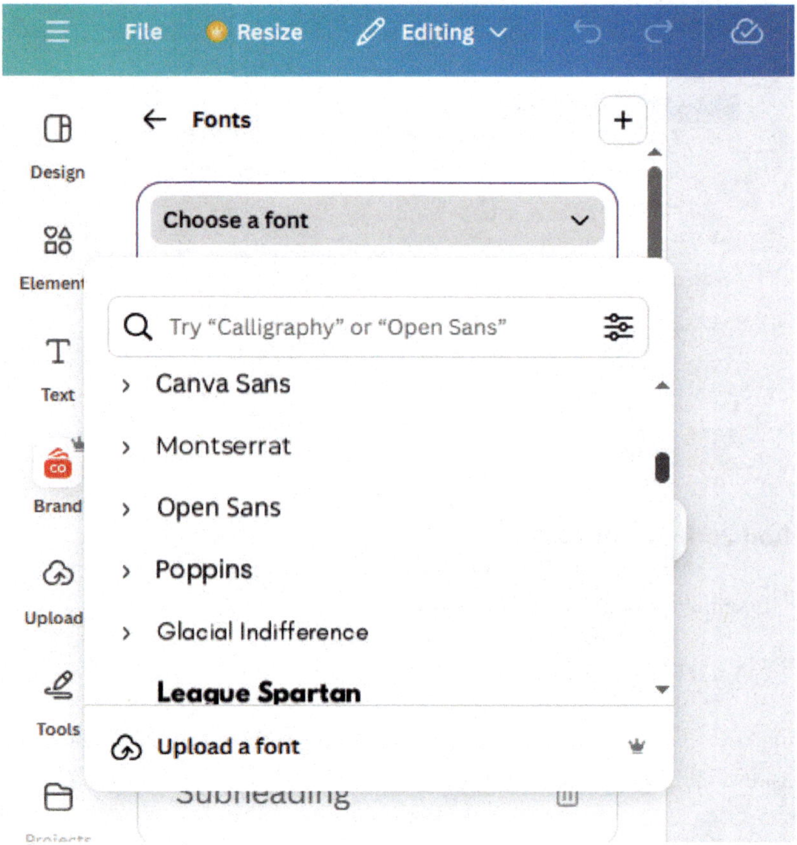

Step 2: Upload Your Font

1. Scroll down to the "Typography" section.
2. Click "Upload a font."
3. Choose a TTF, OTF, or WOFF file from your computer.
4. Click "Yes, upload anyway" if Canva warns you about font licensing.

Step 3: Use Your Uploaded Font

1. Open any design in Canva.

2. Select a text box and click the font dropdown.

3. Scroll down to the "Uploaded fonts" section and choose your font.

Here are a few things to keep in mind when uploading fonts:

- Uploaded fonts are available only to you (or your team if using Canva for Teams).
- Make sure you have the right to use the font commercially.
- Free Canva users cannot upload fonts, but they can use Canva's built-in font library.

Now, you can personalize your designs even further with your unique fonts!

How to Curve Text in Canva

Curving text in Canva is a simple yet effective way to add a creative touch to your designs. You might want to use it while designing a logo, a social media post, or a fun graphic. Here's how to do it:

Step 1: Add Your Text

1. Open Canva and create or open a design.

2. Click on "Text" from the left-side menu.

3. Choose a text style or click "Add a text box."

4. Type in your text and adjust the font, size, and color as needed.

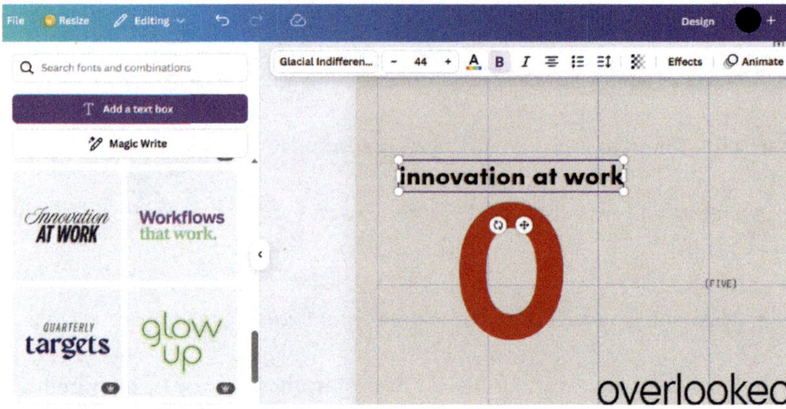

Step 2: Apply the Curve Effect

1. Click on the text box to select it.
2. In the top toolbar, click on "Effects."
3. Scroll down and select "Curve."

Step 3: Adjust the Curve

1. Use the slider to adjust the curve.

    - Drag right to create an upward curve.
    - Drag left to create a downward curve.

2. Fine-tune the letter spacing if needed by clicking "Spacing" in the top menu.

Pro Tips

- Combine curved text with other design elements to create eye-catching logos or badges.
- For a full-circle effect, duplicate the text, curve it in the opposite direction, and align both pieces.
- Experiment with different fonts to see how the curvature affects readability.

Now, go ahead and give your text some stylish curves!

How to Add a Hyperlink in Canva

Let's say you're creating an infographic and want to make certain elements clickable to direct viewers to another page or resource. Canva makes it simple to hyperlink text, images, elements, and even videos.

However, there's one limitation – hyperlinks only work in PDF files. If you're designing a video, links are clickable only in Presenter View, not in the exported video itself.

Here are the steps to add a hyperlink in Canva:

1. **Select the element you want to hyperlink:** This can be text, an image, a shape, or a button.
2. **Use the shortcut for quick linking:** Press Cmd + K (Mac) or Ctrl + K (Windows) to open the hyperlink menu.
3. **Enter the URL:** Type or paste the link you want to attach and hit "Enter" or click "Apply."

4. **Download as a PDF:** Click "Share" > "Download," then select "PDF Standard" to ensure your links remain clickable.

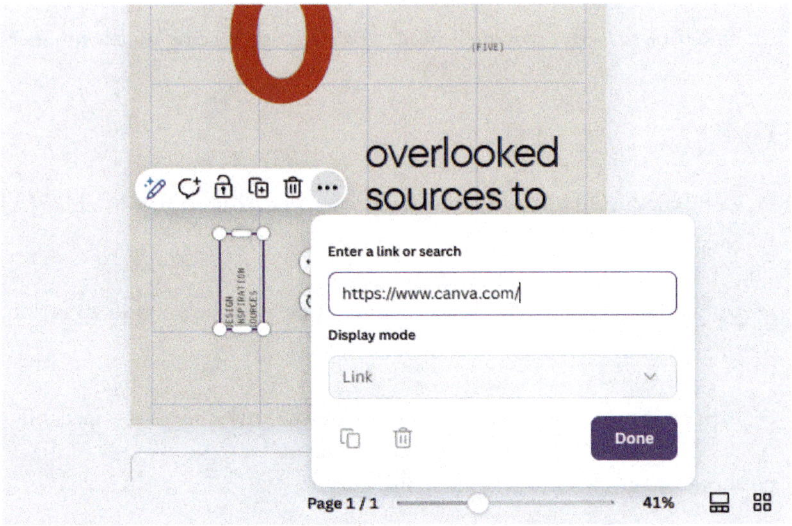

Good to know: If you're creating a multi-page presentation, you can hyperlink elements to different slides within Canva itself.

How to Automatically Resize an Image in Canva

Resizing an image in Canva is quick and easy; however, it is important to know that automatic resizing is a Canva Pro feature, meaning Canva Free users will need to resize manually.

To use Canva's automatic resize feature:

1. **Open your design:** Make sure the image or design you want to resize is selected.

2. **Click on "Resize":** Located in the top menu (only available for Pro users).

3. **Choose preset dimensions:** Select from Canva's suggested sizes for Instagram, Facebook, YouTube, Pinterest, and more.

4. **Click on "Resize" or "Copy and resize":** Resize will adjust your current design, while "Copy and resize" will duplicate it into a new file with the new

dimensions.

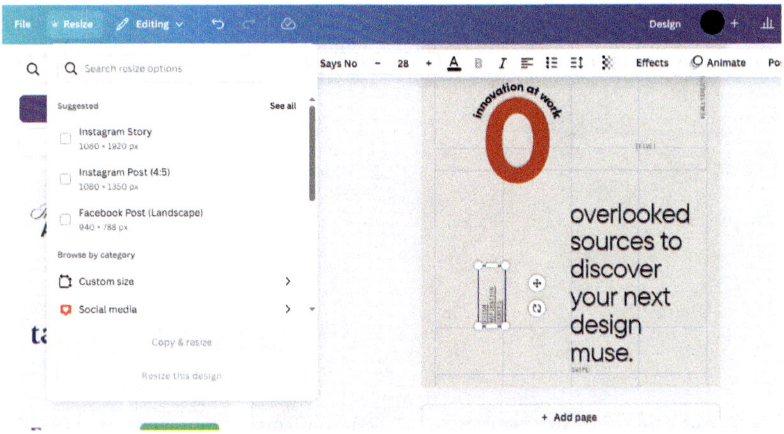

Free users can manually resize their photos by following these steps:

1. Select the image or element and drag the corner handles to resize.
2. Use the "Custom size" option when creating a new design and upload your image again.
3. Adjust the aspect ratio by holding the Shift key while resizing to maintain proportions.

How to Circle Crop an Image in Canva

Want to crop an image into a perfect circle? While there's no direct "Circle crop" button, you can easily achieve this effect using frames. Here's how:

- **Open Canva:** Start a new design or open an existing one.
- **Go to Elements:** On the left panel, search for "Circle frame."

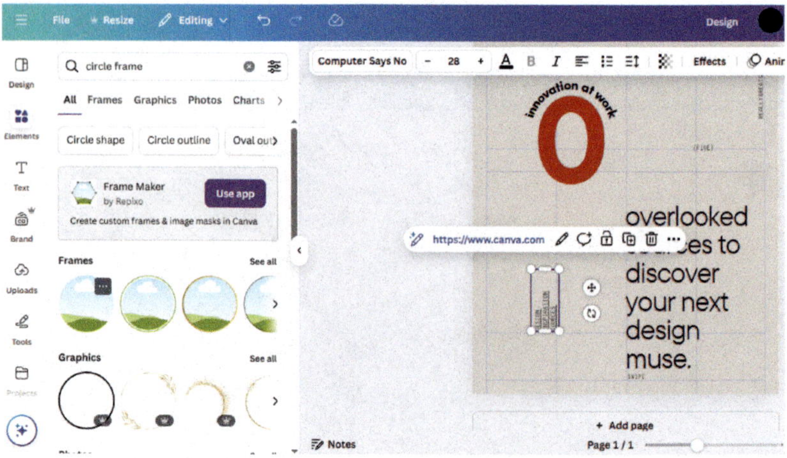

- **Drag and drop the frame:** Select a circular frame and place it on your design.

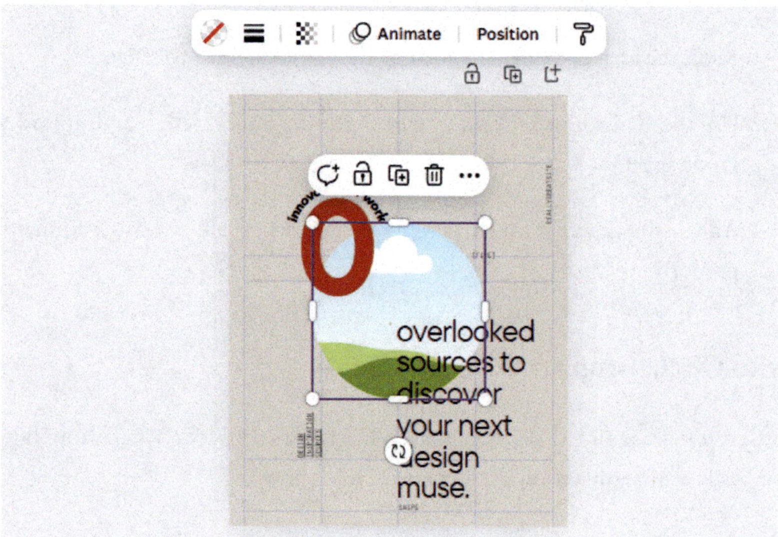

- **Upload or select your image:** Drag your image into the circle frame, and Canva will automatically crop it into the shape.

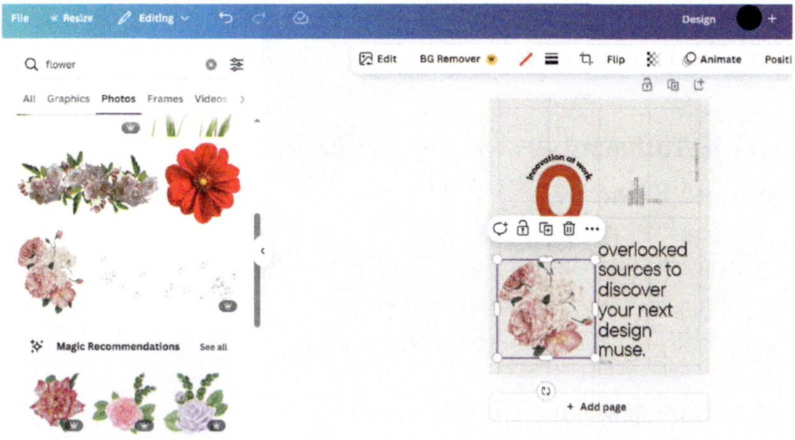

- **Adjust the inside the circle:** Double-click the image inside the frame to reposition or resize it as needed.

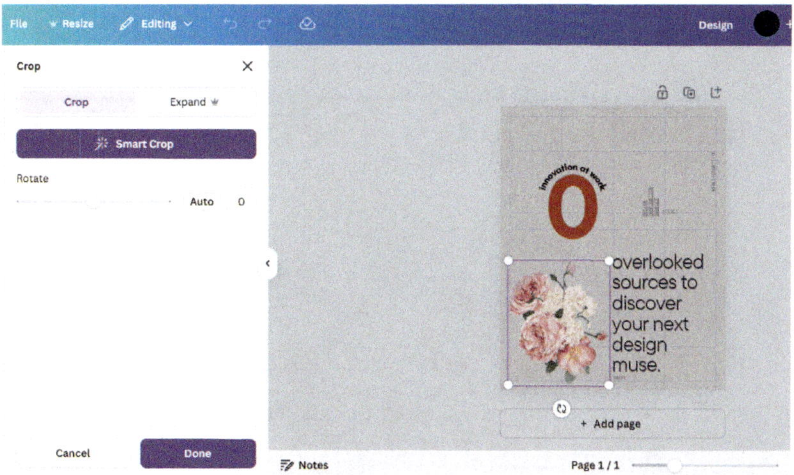

Tip: If you want a border around your cropped image, simply add a second, slightly larger circle behind it in your preferred color!

How to Remove the Background in Canva

Need to remove the background from an image in Canva? If you're using a Canva Pro or Canva for Teams account, you have access to two AI-powered tools that make background removal quick and easy. If you're on a free plan, Canva allows you to try each tool once – so make it count!

Method 1: Automatically Remove the Background With Canva's Background Remover

If you want an effortless way to remove backgrounds, Canva's Background Remover does the heavy lifting for you. This tool instantly identifies and removes the background from your image with just a few clicks. Here's how to use it:

- **Open your design:** Select the image you want to edit.
- **Click on the image:** Make sure it's highlighted in the editor.
- **Select "BG Remover":** This option appears in the top toolbar.
- **Let Canva work its magic:** The background will be removed instantly.

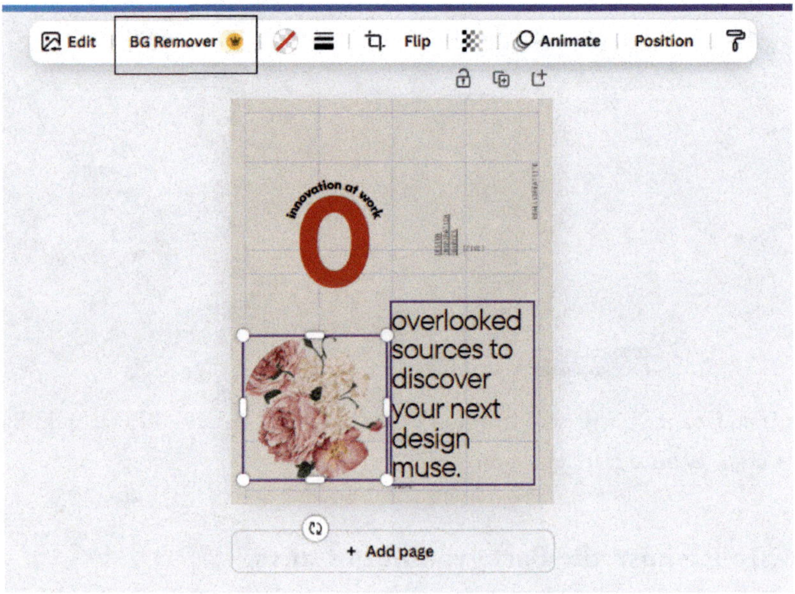

Tip: If parts of the image aren't removed correctly, you can manually refine the edges using the "Erase and restore" tool.

Method 2: Manually Remove Backgrounds With the Magic Eraser

Magic Eraser is your go-to tool if you want more control over which parts of the background to erase. This is perfect for removing unwanted objects without deleting the entire background.

Here is how to use Magic Eraser in Canva:

1. **Open your image in Canva:** Select the design file you want to edit.
2. **Click on the image:** Then, go to Edit in the toolbar.
3. **Find Magic Eraser:** It's under the "Magic Studio" section in the side panel.
4. **Choose your erasing method:**
    - **Brush tool:** Drag the brush over the areas you want to erase. Adjust the brush size for precision.
    - **Click-to-remove:** Simply click on the object or section you want to delete.
5. **Erase and refine:** Once you're happy with the changes, click "Erase" (for the brush) or "Clear" (for object removal).

Tip: If you're removing a background to place the subject onto another background, try adding shadows or adjusting the edges for a seamless effect!

How to Group Elements in Canva

When working on a design in Canva, grouping elements helps you move, resize, and edit multiple objects at once without affecting their alignment. This feature is especially useful when working with text, shapes, icons, or images that need to stay together.

Here's how to group elements using a desktop:

- **Select the elements:** Click and drag your mouse over the objects you want to group, or hold "Shift" and click each element individually.

- **Group the elements:** Click the "Group" button in the top toolbar or use the shortcut:
    - **Mac:** Cmd + G
    - **Windows:** Ctrl + G
- **Move or resize as a group:** Once grouped, you can drag, resize, rotate, or duplicate the elements together.

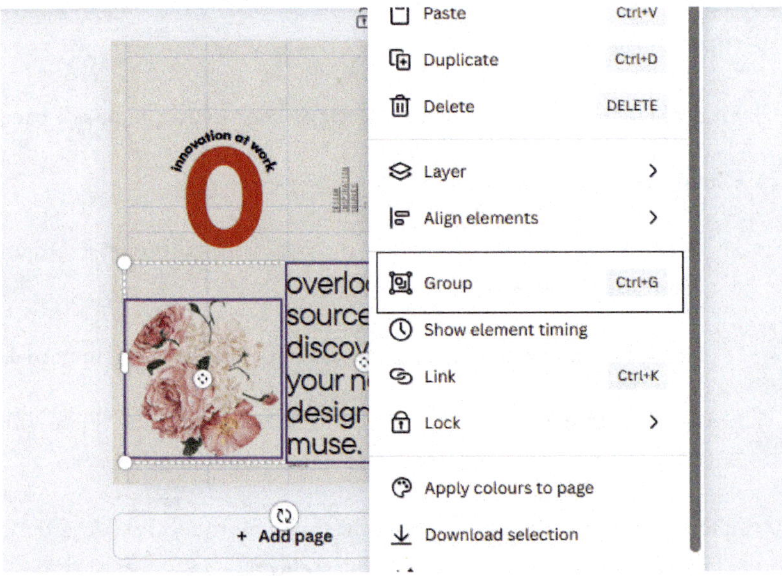

To ungroup elements:

- Select the grouped objects.
- Click "Ungroup" in the top toolbar or use the shortcut:
    - **Mac:** Cmd + Shift + G
    - **Windows:** Ctrl + Shift + G

If you are using a mobile phone to group elements:

1. Tap and hold one element, then tap on additional elements to select them.
2. Look for the "Group" option at the bottom of the screen and tap it.
3. Your selected elements will now be grouped so you can move and resize them together.

Pro Tips for Using Groups in Canva

- **Lock a group:** If you don't want to accidentally move a grouped set, click "Lock" in the toolbar.
- **Nest groups:** Canva allows sub-grouping inside larger groups, so you can group different elements while keeping sections independent.
- **Align and distribute elements before grouping:** To create balanced designs, use Canva's "Align and distribute" tools before grouping.

How to Use Tables in Canva

While Canva doesn't have a built-in table tool like traditional word processors, there are multiple ways to create and customize tables within the platform, but let's take a look at the easiest one:

- Open your Canva design.
- Click on "Elements" in the left sidebar.
- Search for "Table" in the search bar.

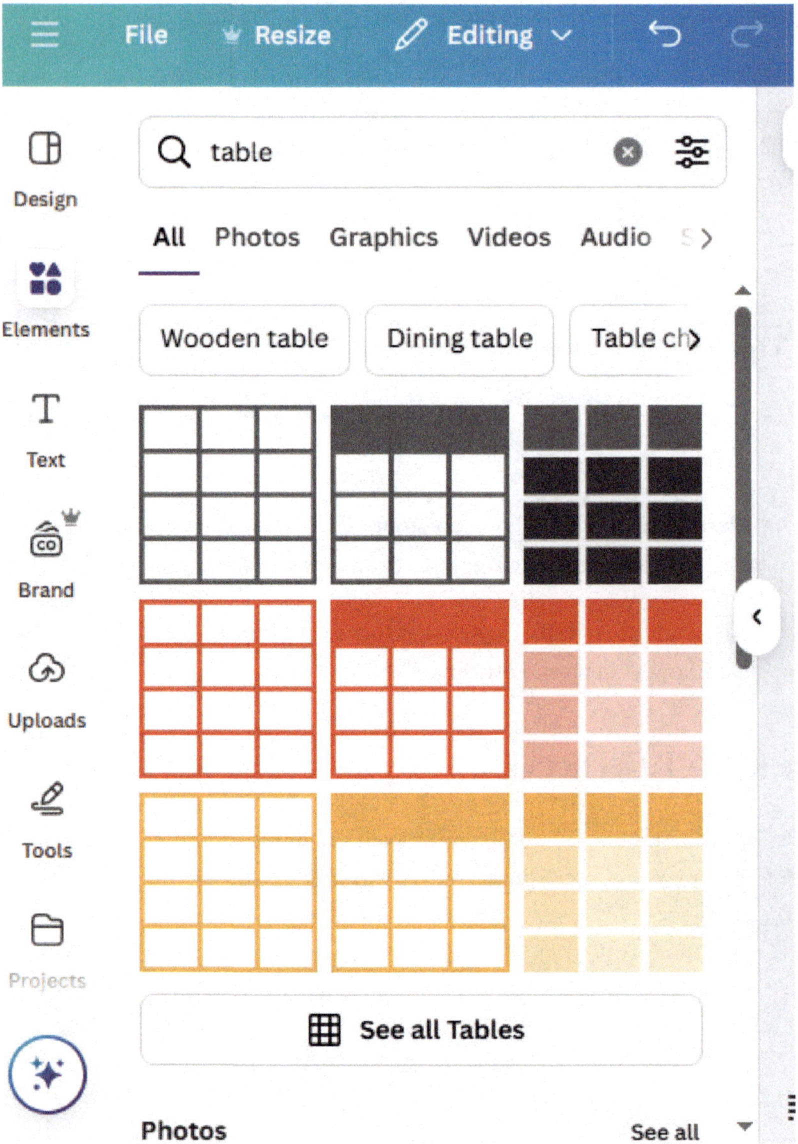

- Click on a table template to add it to your design.
- Adjust the number of rows and columns using the toolbar at the top.
- Customize the colors, borders, and fonts to match your design.

Back to You

By now, we have looked at the most frequently asked questions about using Canva. The best way to learn Canva is to experiment, click around, test out different tools, and don't be afraid to make mistakes. And remember, if you ever get stuck, Canva's Help Center, community forums, and tutorials are great resources to explore!

Now that you're equipped with the answers to some of the most common questions, let's wrap things up and get you ready to create with confidence!

Conclusion

Now that you have mastered the basics, let the creativity flow!

You have made it this far, and now you have a solid foundation for using Canva to create stunning designs, whether for social media, branding, marketing, or personal projects. But the exciting part is that you are only just getting started! Canva is a vast, ever-evolving platform filled with creative possibilities, and the best way to master it is to dive in and start experimenting.

While this book has walked you through the essential tools and techniques, Canva offers so much more beyond the basics. Advanced features like animation effects, interactive presentations, data visualization tools, and even AI-powered design assistants are waiting for you to explore. The beauty of Canva is that it's incredibly user-friendly and allows you to learn as you go.

So, what's the best way to continue learning? Click, experiment, and explore. Try out different templates, play with new design elements, and push your creativity. Don't be afraid to make mistakes, every click teaches you something new.

As you get more comfortable with the basics, start experimenting with advanced tools like Canva's Magic Resize for repurposing designs across multiple platforms, Background Remover for seamless cutouts, and Brand Kit to maintain consistency across all your visuals. Dive into Canva's stock library filled with high-quality photos, illustrations, and videos, or test out collaboration features to streamline teamwork on shared projects.

The more you use Canva, the more confident and creative you'll become. Whether you're designing for personal use, business, or social media, the key is to keep creating. Design is a skill that improves with practice, and Canva makes that process fun, intuitive, and accessible to everyone.

So, go ahead – get click-happy! Open Canva, start a new project, and let your creativity take the lead. Who knows? Your next design might be the one that grabs attention, tells a compelling story, or even helps grow your brand. Happy designing!

Keep Creating with Confidence

You've taken the first step into the world of design and now you're equipped with the tools, tips, and confidence to bring your ideas to life with Canva. If this guide helped you in any way, I'd love for you to share your experience.

Your review helps other beginners discover this book and start their own creative journey. Whether it was the clear steps, real examples, or just feeling less overwhelmed, your honest feedback makes a difference!

Leave a Quick Review

It's simple! Just scan the QR code below.

Whatever stood out to you, your honest review will make a huge difference.

Leave a Review

Write a few sentences about your favorite feature or how this guide helped you feel more confident using Canva!

Thank you for being part of this creative journey. Your voice helps others feel brave enough to start.

– Jules Harper

Bonus!

Yay! You are officially a Canva master now! To kick off your creative journey, check out these fun and fabulous font and color combinations that will make your designs stand out. Your next masterpiece is only a click away!

Font combination to try now	Why they work together
Lato Light + Tenor Sans	a clean and modern pairing with a balance of elegance and readability
Signature + Bodoni FLF	a stylish mix of handwritten script and a bold, classic serif for contrast
Margin + Moontime	combines a contemporary sans-serif with a flowing script for a chic look
Trend Slab One + Stars & Love	a bold slab serif with a decorative, artistic font creates a dynamic effect
Sifonn Outline + Golden	an outlined geometric font paired with a warm, elegant typeface for a sophisticated touch
Lovelo + Billion Miracles	a modern, outlined sans-serif combined with a whimsical script for a creative feel
Brendon + Libre Baskerville	the strong, playful Brendon contrasts beautifully with the classic, readable Libre Baskerville
Billion Miracles + Dream Avenue	two decorative fonts that complement each other for a dreamy, artistic vibe

Color combinations to try now	Best for
Navy Blue + Gold (#1A237E + #FFD700)	luxury branding, high-end products, elegant invitations
Teal + Coral (#008080 + #FF6F61)	modern websites, fashion brands, tropical themes
Black + Neon Green (#000000 + #39FF14)	tech branding, gaming graphics, futuristic designs
Blush Pink + Charcoal (#F4C2C2 + #333333)	beauty brands, wedding invitations, minimalist aesthetics
Mustard Yellow + Deep Purple (#FFC107 + #673AB7)	bold statement graphics, artistic posters, retro vibes
Soft Lavender + Mint Green (#E6E6FA + #98FB98)	wellness brands, spa logos, relaxing aesthetics
Red + Turquoise (#E63946 + #30D5C8)	eye-catching social media posts, dynamic ads, creative branding
Earthy Terracotta + Olive Green (#E2725B + #556B2F)	organic brands, eco-conscious businesses, bohemian designs
Deep Blue + Bright Orange (#003366 + #FFA500)	corporate branding, professional presentations, sports teams
Monochrome Grayscale (#FFFFFF, #808080, #000000)	sleek, modern layouts, high-contrast branding, tech aesthetics

References

Andrews, L. (2021, December 23). *Reflecting on a huge year: 2021 by the numbers.* Canva. https://www.canva.com/newsroom/news/canva-in-numbers-2021/Andrews, L. (2021, December 23). *Reflecting on a huge year: 2021 by the numbers.* Canva. https://www.canva.com/newsroom/news/canva-in-numbers-2021/

Case study on Apple's "Shot on iPhone" brand campaign. (2024, January 7). The Brand Hopper. https://thebrandhopper.com/2024/01/07/a-case-study-on-apples-shot-on-iphone-brand-campaign/

Color theory. (n.d.). Uchicago Library. https://www.lib.uchicago.edu/collex/exhibits/originsof-color/color-theory/

Cummings, C. (2016, April 28). *93% of communication is visual.* LinkedIn. https://www.linkedin.com/pulse/93-communication-visual-carl-cummings/

Gilchrist, K. (2020, January 9). *How a 32-year-old turned a high school yearbook idea into a $3.2 billion business.* CNBC. https://www.cnbc.com/2020/01/09/canva-how-melanie-perkins-built-a-3point2-billion-dollar-design-start-up.html

Harvey, J. (2017, January 3). *Slideology by Nancy Duarte: The art & science of creating great presentations.* Presentation Guru. https://www.presentation-guru.com/slideology-by-nancy-duarte-create-moving-and-amazing-presentations/

Holmes, M. (2021, October 13). *Canva launches video suite to empower everyone to create, edit and record stunning videos.* Canva. https://www.canva.com/newsroom/news/canva-launches-video-suite-empower-everyone-create-edit-record-stunning-videos/

Importance of precision. (2016, May 26). Qualitetch. https://www.qualitetch.com/importance-precision/

Konrad, A. (2019, December 11). *Canva uncovered: How a young Australian kitesurfer built a $3.2 billion (profitable!) startup phenom.* Forbes. https://www.forbes.com/sites/alexkonrad/2019/12/11/inside-canva-profitable-3-billion-startup-phenom/

Nelson, S. (2024, November 6). How to use video content to grow your business. *Forbes.* https://www.forbes.com/councils/forbesbusinesscouncil/2024/11/06/how-to-use-video-content-to-grow-your-business/

Pearce, J. C. (n.d.). *Joseph Chilton Pearce quotes.* Goodreads. http://goodreads.com/author/quotes/30099.Joseph_Chilton_Pearce

Use Magic Design to create a video. (n.d.). Canva. https://www.canva.com/help/using-magic-video/

Images

TheDigitalArtist. (2016, October 17). *Color wheel* [Image]. Pixabay. https://pixabay.com/illustrations/colour-wheel-spectrum-rainbow-1740381/

Printed in Dunstable, United Kingdom

80782301R00067